To: Greg & Mary ~

Our Stories are everything.

NICOLE DONOVAN

A LIFE SUSPENDED

A Mother and Son's Story of Autism,
Extinction Bursts, and Living a
Resilient Life.

SOVEREIGN QUEEN PRESS

Donovan, Nicole

A Life Suspended: A Mother and Son's Story of Autism, Extinction Bursts, and Living a Resilient Life / Nicole Donovan

Summary: A mother lives through the highs and lows of having a child with Autism, and the journey it sets her on as a mother, wife, and woman.

ISBN: 978-1-7346286-0-9

SOVEREIGN QUEEN PRESS

Published in the United States of America

For all the families navigating this journey, know with certainty you are not alone. For our "first responders," the ones who answered the call, rolled up their sleeves and got into the trenches with us. Your dedication and steadfast belief in Jack carried us during our darkest days. Your expertise gave us a blueprint to build a strong foundation, one we all rely on to this day. We are forever grateful.

For my husband Mike, whose love and support has meant everything.

And for Jack, whose resilience has been a powerful example of recovery, acceptance and self-love. May your story provide inspiration for others and for them to see the world from a slightly different perspective.

CONTENTS

PRAISE FOR NICOLE DONOVAN

"While this book is about motherhood, education and navigating many of life's challenges and inequities, it's actually a deep reflection on our interconnectedness and humanity. Nicole courageously walks us through her journey of advocacy with humor, love and grace. She brings a vulnerability and strength that is more than just inspiration and education - though there's plenty of both - it's a story of becoming."

- Janell Burley Hofmann, Author of iRules, International Speaker, Facilitator and Consultant, Mother of 5

"This book is raw, vulnerable and relatable. Donovan's use of descriptive language invites you into their unique world of autism. By telling her story she gives parents hope, and helps others understand the complexities families face in navigating the special education system. As a parent, an educator and special education advocate, this book is an essential read for any parent of a child learns differently."

- Tricia Moore, Educational Advocate, Mother of two

"Just as Temple Grandin provided us insight into living in a world as a person with autism, Nicole Donovan is now lending voice to families that have children with autism. In *A Life Suspended*, Ms. Donovan has given a gracious and generous invitation to experience the joys and heartache captured in this brilliant snapshot of her family album. As educators, as well as clinicians, we would be remiss not to accept her invitation and use it as an opportunity to gain insight from a family perspective.

This should be required reading for all those entering the field. Jack's story is a reminder to all who work with children in schools that we have a responsibility to be honest and forth-coming in our observations. Our words and actions devoid of empathy and compassion leave long lasting imprints. As Ms. Donovan so poignantly captures in her story, whatever we do and whatever we say, every student is someone's child and deserve to be treated as such. Thank you for sharing your journey as a parent and Jack's journey as your son."

~ *Debra Edgren, M. Ed., C.A.G.S., School Psychologist*

"This is a tender story of love and awareness. I wondered as a child free woman if I would be able to resonate with a mother's story of raising an autistic son...As I read the last page, closed this book and held it to my heart to absorb its wisdom. I was so proud of Jack. He is the hero of this story and it was an absolute honor to witness his unique road to freedom...I feel everyone will benefit from the universal nuggets of grace sprinkled throughout the telling of this beautiful story of resilience and surrender."

~ *Sheree Asdot, Certified Hypnotherapist, Reiki Master*

THE ESCAPE

"Things have regressed significantly since this morning."

I identified the familiar voice of Jack's school vice principal and glanced up at the clock on the wall. It had been two hours since her last phone call. It was 12:25 p.m., and below the clock sat my fifteen preschool students, who were happily chatting and eating their lunches. I motioned to my co-teacher, signaling to her that I needed to take the call.

"Well," she continued. "Last we spoke, Jack had been removed from the classroom due to another violent outburst which included clearing his desk and whipping his coat at his teacher. As you know, this was a full day removal—an in-house suspension," she paused.

She explained that Jack's one-to-one aide had taken him into the conference room to do his classroom assignments, but Jack became upset and kicked the door as they were entering the room and it swung and hit the aide in his elbow, and the aide needed to leave to get medical attention. Jack's aide had been recently assigned to him when things began to escalate. My son's intolerance to his academics had increased and staying on task had become very challenging for him. When his educational team met several weeks prior, they thought that having a one-to-one support would help him manage the class time better, but it turned out not to be the case. Instead, Jack was given the opportunity to leave the classroom whenever he felt challenged. If he acted poorly—he would be removed.

Jack was left in the care of the vice principal during lunch. When she turned around to open the window in her office, Jack bolted. He had run out of the building and down the street. She radioed for help and the social worker ran outside after him. Unfortunately, the social worker fell on the sidewalk and injured his hand and broke a tooth. When the social worker reached Jack, he was being held by a passer-by. A man driving in a pick-up truck two blocks down from the school had noticed he was running away from the school, and being so young, he stopped him.

My seven-year-old son was running away from school and a complete stranger caught him.

As I drove across town, I called my husband. The first thing I told him was that Jack was physically fine. Then I shared the conversations I'd had with the vice principal. As I replayed her words, I remembered something she'd said to me earlier that morning. After she explained that Jack was removed from his classroom and would be placed in a separate room for the day, she said that she wasn't sure how that would go and specifically labeled Jack as a flight risk.

"Do you think she *let* him go?" I asked Mike. My voice was shaking.

"I don't think a professional would do that. What if something happened to him? The liability would be insurmountable," my husband assured me. I could hear he was trying to convince himself almost as much as he was trying to convince me. Mike had always been able to cut through things with a clear and concise focus—the gift of a logical mind.

"Do you want me to come to the school and meet you?"

"No, I don't think I'll be there long."

Mike was all the way in Boston, more than an hour's drive from our little Cape Cod town.

Arriving at the school, I entered both sets of double doors, walked into the school foyer and up to the office window. The school secretary, who had seen me a million times at this window with trays of cookies for bake sales, school plays, or PTA meetings, barely spoke to me. She knew me. She knew all four of my children. Over the years, we had woven ourselves into the fabric that made this community shine. Today, however, her greeting was cool and impersonal. Her words were blunt and short.

I walked down to the vice principal's office. Jack was sitting at a rectangular work desk with his backpack and jacket. He appeared happy to see me, but there was hardness to his face. His eyes darted over to the vice principal then back to me.

I asked him if he was all right, and he nodded.

"Jack, you know that it's not safe to leave school like that. We were so worried about you."

He looked at me and said, "I was going home. I was on the

sidewalk being safe. I would have made it home all by myself! Can we leave now?" Exasperated, he crossed his arms sharply.

Even through his tough demeanor, I saw him. His deep blue eyes, framed by his angry brow, told a story. They told me that he was scared and frustrated and lost. His caramel-colored hair styled into a boy's regular, reminded me of his tender age, and his pink cheeks allowed me to see the softness of him.

She could see him too, right?

I WAS ASKED to speak to the principal. As I waited outside of her office, I could see through the thin, tall rectangular window embedded in the door, Mr. Rafferty, the Head of Pupil Personnel for our school district. We knew Mr. Rafferty as the principal at The Bradford School, prior to being appointed to this new position. At the time, I remember wondering why the title had changed from Head of Special Education to Head of Pupil Personnel when he took the job. Later, it was revealed that it was due to the fact that he did not hold a degree in special education; his credentials could not uphold the title the way it was written, so they changed the title.

A familiar teacher that my son had a couple of years ago nodded as she passed by. Her smile was laced with sympathy, her eyes lowered quickly to the corridor floor. With all the commotion, everyone knew about Jack, or about the boy who eloped from school. Maybe they remembered he was the same kid who ran out of the school six weeks ago—who'd left right in the middle of their morning work cycle, out the door, down the first-grade hallway, and out of the building? Or maybe they knew he was the kid who cleared his teacher's desk and called the vice principal a "bitch?" There were several incidences over the past two months at school.

The principal's door opened, and Mr. Rafferty walked out.

"Hello, Mrs. Donovan," he said and extended his arm to shake my hand. "Bob Rafferty, head of pupil personnel."

His palm was moist, and his face was the color of ash. Although, he looked me in the eye, his gaze quickly fell to the worn checkered linoleum tiles below me.

"Yes, Bob, I remember you," I said trying to catch his eye.

"She will be speaking with you now, but I will be in touch soon."

And with that, he turned and walked away. Were his pants on fire? Was that why he was practically running down the hall?

The principal guided me into her room and offered me a seat. I could tell she was anxious; her hands were twisting around each other as she spoke about Jack. She explained step by step what had happened, her words quick. At times she sounded breathless.

She ended by saying, "Mr. Rafferty and I met to discuss Jack. He will be meeting with the superintendent to come up with an alternative educational setting. We don't think that we can keep Jack safe here."

Can't keep Jack safe here. What?

She continued, "I don't know what the offer will be, but until then, we don't feel that Jack should be here at school."

Did they just kick my son out of school? My heart was pounding.

There was a knock at the door; it opened to a husky female police officer in full uniform.

"Mrs. Donovan? I am Officer Kelly. I am the truant officer at

Burbridge High School. They called me when Jack escaped from the building."

After she introduced herself, she positioned her body in front of me, as I sat in the chair looking up at her. With her hands on her hips she began to ask questions. I presumed that we were going to try to get to the bottom of this, of why my 7-year-old son was running away from school. But as the questions rolled on, instead of feeling supported, I felt interrogated.

"I heard that your son has been removed several times from the classroom and has physically assaulted teachers at school," she said.

Physically assaulted?

"Your son hit employees here at the school and if he was out in the real world, this would be considered assault. I would have to take him in," she responded as though she'd read my mind. "Has he ever run away from home before?" she asked, eyebrow raised, looking for me to answer.

I tried to decipher her words in my head, and to remember if there was a time Jack ever ran from home.

"No, not that I can recall." I blurted out as I looked up at her, she was slightly swaying back and forth, hands still on her hips, gun holstered.

"Does he have any siblings?" she asked.

"Yes, he has three older brothers." I said quickly.

"Do I *know* any of his brothers?"

I sunk lower into the hard-plastic chair. I felt examined and squeezed. Why would she *know* any of my boys?

"No, I don't think so. He has an older brother Patrick at the high school, but he has never been in trouble."

Officer Kelly turned back to the principal, who was seated

next to me and said, "We can take this as far as CHINS if we need to."

She jumped in and said, "No, that won't be necessary. These are good parents. A good family." She looked alarmed by what the officer had said, the implications that it made, even though I hadn't the slightest knowledge of what "CHINS" was until I got home and Googled it. In the state of Massachusetts, a Child in Need of Services, or "CHINS," is an act that was put in place to help families who have children who run away from home or school. The Massachusetts Juvenile Court helps parents and school officials deal with this issue by enlisting the help of the Department of Family Services, the court system, and probation officers to monitor the child's attendance at school, etc. This seemed to be geared for older children, who were chronic school skippers or had brushes with the law. Not my Jack.

I was awash in feelings of sadness, shame and anger, the emotions interlacing themselves into a rope around my neck. I felt guilty Jack was causing such a commotion at school. I felt sad that staff was unintentionally hurt because Jack was hell-bent on leaving. Sadness gave way to shame... I felt shamed by the officer who was implying that Jack's problems stemmed from the home—from us—from me. This, in turn, made me angry.

"I WOULD LIKE to talk to Jack. Is he still here?" Officer Kelly asked looking at both of us.

"Ah, yes, he is across the hall with the vice principal," said the principal. Her eyes shifted to me she asked, "If it's all right with Mrs. Donovan, of course?" she gestured.

I was paralyzed. What I wanted to say was, *No fucking way.*

We were done here. But, I didn't. She was a police officer, and I had been taught to cooperate and be helpful—particularly with authority figures. I came from a good family. And so did Jack.

I agreed to a quick meeting between Jack and the officer. Jack was looking at one of his favorite Dr. Seuss books, *The Lorax*. He looked up as we came into the room. His eyes digested us: the principal, his mother, and the uniformed police officer. His eyes lingered on Officer Kelly as he watched her walk over to the table and sit diagonally across from him. I sat next to Jack and the principal took the remaining chair. The vice principal hung back near her desk but stayed in the room.

Officer Kelly introduced herself to Jack and began to tell him why she was there. His eyes scanned her uniform and her badge. She talked about safety and rules. She continued to tell him that leaving school was against the rules and that he could get lost.

Jack rebutted forcefully, "I was fine. I was going home using the sidewalk. I would have made it if they didn't stop me." His arms crossed his chest, brow furrowed.

"People got hurt chasing after you," she explained. "They were concerned for your safety, Jack."

"I was safe! I just wanted to go home and be with my Mom. I don't like school."

I saw his eyes find her holster and her gun. Perched on his seat in a catcher's crouch, he shifted his weight in the chair, leaned forward into the table, his eyes were slightly strained. I knew this look. His inquisitive nature was spinning inside his head. Questions were forming and, with his level of unpredictability, I was unsure if he would try to touch the gun, which would alarm everyone.

I abruptly explained that we needed to leave, which cut off

any further discussion. I diverted Jack's focus from the officer's accessories to collect his backpack. We left the officer and two principals behind and even bypassed the office to sign out. I was beginning to understand what Jack might have felt when he ran from the building.

2

UNSCRIPTED

*A*fter turning my car out of the school parking lot, I looked into the rear-facing mirror, and I saw Jack sitting quietly looking out the window. His face was peaceful, no knitted brow or frowned mouth, just contentment as he sat there and looked out into the world. I heard his dangling legs swish back and forth against the back seat. Where do we go now? What do we do? Do I drive him home? Did he eat lunch? Should I take him to McDonalds? Wait. I can't do that. That would be like rewarding him. He just got kicked out of school, I can't reward him for that. No Happy Meal. No Hot Wheels toy prize. I continued driving home while I searched for familiar signs of normalcy. What had happened at the school, the wreckage I found myself wading in, was devastating.

I made the left onto our street and noticed crocuses blooming in one of my neighbor's flowerbeds. Their brightness cut through the muted gray dinginess of its surroundings. Purple, white and yellow rested upon chartreuse stalks, which announced that spring was coming to Cape Cod after all. It was March 20th and while spring was declaring her arrival, instead of feeling filled with joy and hope, I felt panicked. We pulled into the driveway and into our garage. Jack opened the van door slider and jumped out, leaving his backpack behind. I grabbed it along with my own lunch bag and work tote and went into the house. I kept to the tasks at hand: hanging things up, putting things away, making him lunch, cleaning the kitchen counters. My body moved through the motions as my mind tumbled through the day's events. Once Jack was settled watching TV, I dialed the phone and let Mike know we were home.

I began to explain what had happened. My words came out fast and jumbled. I stopped, took a breath, and reset. As I slowed down, and focused, the story became clearer and easier to follow. Mike's initial reaction was anger. He was upset at the school and even more bothered by the way I was treated by the police officer. After a few choice words, he caught himself.

"Are you okay?" his tone softened.

"I am okay, just worried," I exhaled. My voice crackled and tears began to flow down my cheeks.

"It will be okay. We will figure this out together. Jack will be fine. We both know he is nearly indestructible," he said, trying to make the conversation lighter. I nodded silently, afraid if I did open my mouth, I would sob instead.

"Remember him and Aidan rolling down the driveway in the old wagon?"

"Death trap," I said, confirming the memory.

"Yes, death trap, the plastic wagon built for kids that had sides that would, without warning, give way. How many times do you think that kid tumbled out and came up looking to go again?"

"Go again! Go again!" he'd yell as he climbed back in.

"Hundreds?" Mike said, responding to his own question.

It was true. We had often joked about Jack's fearless feats. And on another day, it would bring a smile to my face, solace to my heart, but not today.

I HUNG up the phone with Mike and rested the receiver in my lap. We had agreed that reaching out for professional help would be a good place to start, as this situation was uncommon ground. But who do I call? I wondered. Faces of friends and family scanned through my mind. I came across my friend, Mallory, who had a child with disabilities that attended the same school district as our kids. She often spoke about the challenges of obtaining services for her son.

I left a message on her cell, exhaled, and fell back onto the bed. I lay there, unplugged. I stared blankly at the ceiling, utterly exhausted. I heard the sounds of the television program Jack was watching and his voice talking over it. I strained to hear if anyone was downstairs with him, but there were no other words, only his, echoed up the staircase and through my bedroom door left ajar.

My baby, my sweet, sweet boy.

What were we going to do? A tidal wave of sadness crashed into me, my body tingled with fear, and I began to sob. I moved to shut the door, not wanting Jack to hear me cry. I buried my face in a pillow, completely surrendering to my emotions of powerlessness. Tears soaked my pillow. I tossed it aside and reached for the tissues.

I glanced at the clock; it was almost three o'clock. Kieran, our 7th grader, would be home soon. Patrick, our oldest child and in high school, would be home after Ultimate Frisbee practice. I walked into the master bathroom and looked at my puffy reflection. I ran the faucet, splashed cold water onto my face, and pulled a brush through my hair.

I stood in the doorway of the living room and watched Jack. He lay on the couch with Gigi, his baby blanket, which he liked to sleep and snuggle with. He was watching Mickey Mouse Playhouse, his body still, which was rare, Gigi nestled under his chin in his cupped hands. It was hard to believe this boy was capable of creating such turmoil. This boy, who cleared his teacher's desk and had been suspended twice from school. This boy who ran. This boy who hurt people. Jack might have been fearless, but he was never destructive or harmful. Until now.

He saw me standing there and smiled. I walked over and sat next to him. His eyes returned to Mickey and his cast of characters, only meeting with mine briefly. Years of us physically turning his head so he could "look at me" had helped, but he continued to struggle with eye contact.

Jack had been diagnosed just before his third birthday with a language and processing delay. Other evaluations and diagnoses followed: an ADHD diagnosis from neuropsychological testing and Dyspraxia, along with Sensory Processing Disorder (SPD), at six.

I wanted to reach out and touch him. I wanted to gather him up and squeeze him tight, but I didn't. At the moment, I was unsure of how to parent him.

The clock began to chime, and a new Disney program was about to start, a perfect time to turn off the television before he became engrossed in the next show. We had a few minutes before his brothers would come home from school.

"Jack, can you tell me about today? About what happened at school?" I asked, my body shifted toward him, my eyes at his profile. He remained focused on the blackened screen. A stiff silence filled the room. Jack moved his beloved Gigi up to his face and gave it a sniff.

"Jack, did you hear me?" I asked him, moving my hand to touch his leg, hoping to gain his attention. "Why did you run away from school today? Did something happen?"

His head turned and eyes darted sharply at me, his body became rigid, a drastic change from its softness moments ago.

"I told you already! I wanted to go home. I wanted to do what I wanted to do," he said as his head snapped back toward the darkened television. He began searching for the remote, which had fallen between the couch cushions.

"Jack, wait a minute, we need to talk about this. Are you okay? Did something happen to make you run away?" I pleaded. All I wanted was a sliver from him, something to help me make sense of it all.

"Where is that remote? Ah, here it is!" His fingers fumbled to find the right button.

I placed my hands over the remote, gently wrapping them around his. He jerked them back and glanced at me, looking frustrated and angry.

"I wanted to come home, okay? To do what I want to do. I don't like school! Everyone is always touching me. I don't like them touching me!"

Click. The television was back on. My mind was trying to decipher what he meant by "touching me." I knew that he had been placed in a one-to-one hold several weeks ago by the special education teacher after he had punched the substitute aide who was filling in. He'd had a meltdown and had to be restrained. I didn't know of any other times. I resisted the urge to comfort him. I was afraid that if I reached for him, he would push me away, and the tender part inside of me couldn't bear that.

Jack was the baby of our family. The adventurous boy-wonder who loved nothing more than to be surrounded by his three older brothers, or to climb to the highest rungs on the monkey bars, or to knock on our neighbor's door and invite himself in for a cup of juice and a snack. He was bold and zest-ful. Distracted and driven. His expression of love was both fierce and endearing, often hurling his body into mine for hugs and kisses. He laughed wildly, without reservation. He was joyful and filled with life. But, in recent months I had watched his light slowly dampen. I felt a tear trickle down my cheek and looked away from Jack.

MY THOUGHTS WERE INTERRUPTED by the slamming of the door. Kieran was home. *Thud.* I heard his backpack hit the mudroom floor and thunderous clomp of his shoes as they tumbled into the boot tray. I stood up and straightened my blouse, trying to pull myself together.

"OH, hi Mom. I didn't know you were home. Is Jack here?" He nodded his head toward the living room.

"Yeah, Jack is here."

"Oh. Is he okay? I heard that he left school today. All the kids were talking about it." He said as he moved toward the refrigerator.

"Yes, he is fine. A bit shaken up, but fine. At this point, I'm not sure what is going on. He won't be returning to Bradford."

"What do you mean? Did he get kicked out of school?" he asked. His hazel eyes flashed a look of concern. Kieran was a sensitive kid. Although he didn't articulate it, I felt the vibration of Kieran's alarm bell sounding for his younger brother.

"I don't know. That's what we are going to figure out," I said cautiously. "Did any of your teachers or school staff pull you aside to talk to you today? To let you know what was going on with Jack?" I asked.

"Nope. I just heard rumors from the kids in my grade. And you know Ben's mom is a first-grade teacher, so he told me what he knew. I wasn't sure what to believe."

I leaned against the kitchen counter and watched his profile as he ate his snack at the table. No one spoke to him? Kieran had spent half of his day hearing rumors about his little brother, all the chatter and drama filling the halls of the teenage section of the school. Did administration not think that my other boys would hear about it?

The rest of the kids filed in, Aidan, our third grader who was at a friend's house after school and Patrick who had been at a meeting for Ultimate Frisbee. Mike had just called. He was making his way home from Boston and while traffic was moving, he was still a half an hour away from home. I looked into the fridge to see what I could pull together for dinner. Leftover meatballs and sauce—perfect! I grabbed a box of pasta from the cabinet. *This* I can do. *This* made sense. I could organize meals on the fly, keep track of backpacks and lunch money, laundry and school supplies. I excelled at multitasking. I thrived when I was busy, with many of moving parts to my day. I'd end up exhausted but satisfied. My life was ordered and structured. I'd do the *next* thing. There was *always* a *next* thing. Possibly two, or three, *next* things…Now, with Jack, there was stagnancy. Lack of motion. Uncertainty.

The kids and I were halfway through dinner when Mike arrived, briefcase in hand. He quickly dropped his things and squeezed into a spot at our rectangular kitchen table. The chatter seemed like normal weeknight dinner—Aidan talked about his day, his whole day, from when he woke to present, making sure he filled us in on every detail. Patrick was on his second helping of pasta after inhaling the first round. Kieran was quiet, possibly contemplating his next sarcastic remark about Aidan's day. Those two were like oil and water. And Jack, who refused to eat pasta due to its texture, struggled to cut up his meatballs with a knife and fork. Mike gestured to Jack, modeling the proper way to hold the utensils, hoping that Jack would catch on. He tried but became frustrated and cut the balls into large chunks, which he ate off his fork. Mike let it go, probably realizing that eating like a semi-domesticated caveman was the least of our worries.

After dinner and dessert were eaten and the younger boys were tucked into their beds, Mike and I sat in the family room, while Patrick and Kieran were in the living room playing on the computer. I glanced over at him, his face drained, body sunken into the caramel colored couch. He rubbed his face with his hands.

"I called and left a message for Mallory. I know she has an

17

educational advocate that she has used for years," I said, trying to muster a tone of hopefulness.

"Well, our situation may be beyond hiring an advocate. We might need someone with a bigger hand to deal with Jack's current situation," he said in a low voice, not to be overheard. "A lawyer," he said, to make sure we were on the same page.

Helpless and brokenhearted, we sat for a while in stillness and sifted through the events of the day and the days before, trying to piece it all together. We tried to make sense of where we were and where we were going, until we realized we had come full circle. Our wheels were spinning, and no resolution was going to happen that night.

"Let's see if we hear from them tomorrow. You'll be home with Jack and if you can follow up on getting names and gathering some information that would be great."

"Okay. I can do that," I said.

Well, I guess I just found the *next* thing...

3

PAPER TRAIL OF SELF-DOUBT

*J*ack came into this world like a rocket ship. In the wee hours of the morning on the Saturday after Thanksgiving, Mike drove me to the hospital. It wasn't a leisurely drive. Instead, it was like a scene out of the movie *The Ballad of Ricky Bobby*, where his father is racing to the hospital while his wife was at the end stages of labor in the backseat. Yup, that was me. Jack was my fourth child and what I thought was false labor the evening before, wasn't. As soon as we got into the car, I felt the urge to push. As I mentioned this to Mike, he responded by saying, "No, you don't! Just breathe through the contractions. We'll be at the hospital soon."

With no one on the road and Mike putting the car into warp speed we made record time. At the emergency room entrance, we abandoned the car and an attendant placed me in a wheelchair. As we arrived on the labor and delivery floor, we bypassed the woman at the registration desk as I yelled, "No time! No time!" I couldn't even put my bottom on the seat of the wheelchair because Jack's head was crowning. The doors burst open on the ward and bodies in pastel scrubs met me and Mike and ushered us quickly into the birthing room. They helped me stand up and nursing staff pulled off my sweatpants and underwear. I fell onto the hospital bed and three short pushes later, Jack was born.

Jack was no worse for wear, a perfect little package. All his scores were well within the normal range. He was to be our last child, completing our family at six. My heart expanded once more, enveloping the essences of this powerhouse of a being, knowing he was going to do just fine as the youngest of four boys.

Over the years, Mike described coming home after a long day at work when the kids were ten and under, reminiscent of a scene from the Muppet Movie, where Kermit, Fozzie and Gonzo arrived at the Happiness Hotel and were greeted by a collection of Muppet characters hanging from the rafters singing. At the time, I had a family home daycare, so we had a few extra "Muppets" running around.

In those younger years, Jack wrestled with his brothers, grunted for more juice and climbed anything that wasn't nailed down. When we moved to Cape Cod, I decided to take a couple of years off from working to enjoy being a mom.

In Burbridge, our sleepy little town on Cape Cod, one of Jack's favorite activities was attending story hour with Mr. Peters at the Burbridge Public Library. It was a popular sign-up for toddler- and preschool-aged children alike and Mr. Peters was the pied piper. He was magnetic. Jack didn't suffer from separation anxiety or have any fear of going into a group of people. In fact, he often would plow through the seated children and plop himself right down. He wasn't being intentionally rude; in fact, he didn't appear to have any awareness that his body was bouncing into other kids as he made his way toward the front of the carpeted area. He was solely focused on sitting with Mr. Peters.

When Mr. Peters read, he'd stop and ask questions, often pointing to the illustrations to engage the group. When appropriate, he called on children by name. Sometimes, he would forget one of the kid's names, but never Jack's. He remembered his name because Jack was literally in front of his face. In a sea of twenty children sitting on the floor, Jack popped up to answer Mr. Peters when he posed a question to the crowd. Jack was so intently focused on his buddy, everything else faded away. He didn't notice other children around him or take any social cues.

Jack attended the preschool story hour where the kids were older. Nobody in this crowd jumped up, pressed their index finger into the pages of the book and answered loudly, "Green frog!" when Mr. Peters read, *Brown Bear, Brown Bear* by Bill Martin, Jr. and Eric Carle. On a couple of occasions, I removed Jack from story time, not because he was asked to leave, but because he was overriding the show. He was unaware he was stepping over the social boundaries of the group and others began to notice. *Moms* began to notice. I felt uncomfortable as I felt their judgment skim over me as I sat on the edge of the circle. I tried to have Jack sit with me, but after he was pulled from prime seating up front, he wouldn't settle down. We tried another session of story time, but Jack resisted sitting next me or listening to my redirections. It became frustrating for both of us. The last one he attended, I carried Jack out in a football hold with both of us in tears. *Maybe a smaller circle time setting would work?* I thought as I drove out of the library parking lot.

. . .

I LEAFED through the file box that housed all of Jack's previous evaluations—preschool reports, observations, and Jack's first IEP (Individualized Education Plan). As I shuffled through, a name tag fell free into my lap. My heart melted upon seeing his rosy cheeks, baby-toothed smile and bright blue eyes. *JACK.* It was his name tag from the integrated public preschool program he'd attended for two years after our move to Cape Cod. These picture name cards were located on a large board near the front of the classroom. Each student upon arrival found their name tag and posted it on the "schoolhouse" on the other side of the board. I remembered that Jack needed to be redirected almost daily to get this accomplished. Even though this task sounded simple enough, there were several steps to complete it, and, having an understanding of his sensitivity to large chaotic environments, too much visual stimulation, and noise, it became clearer why he needed additional prompts to be successful.

When we moved to Burbridge in the spring of 2006, I took time off from work and focused on getting settled into our new home and community. The oldest boys began school at Bradford Elementary, Patrick in third grade and Kieran in first. In September, Aidan went to a preschool program, leaving me to have Jack all to myself. We took full advantage of the wonderful local offerings at the public library, parks, beaches, nature walks, and play groups, and on colder days we had a membership to the Cape Cod Children's Museum. Jack loved going to the museum to play, particularly on cold days in the winter and spring. The best part of the Children's Museum was the train table. They had different trains than we did at home. Jack's favorite pastime was building tracks and driving the engines with lots of cars and cargo trailing behind. At home, I'd see him in our living room lying belly on the floor, watching the wheels turn around and round. It felt like time stopped, while the wheels moved. As if he was mesmerized by the engineering of it. But then his gaze broke and his attention was diverted to add more track. He would independently play like this for a long time.

Jack was always a curious and daring child. He had three older brothers to watch and learn from. This was good and bad. He was generally a happy infant—busy, occupied, and entertained by those around him. Jack always wanted to be in the thick of it and be around other kids. By the time we moved to Cape Cod, Jack was totally mobile. We found him on tables and counters, and he scaled the outside of the staircase almost daily. But the kitchen was his favorite room. Pots, pans and deep cabinets filled with food were at the top of his list. I "lost" Jack a few times inside our new home as he found new closets or nooks to hide in. At eighteen months, Jack pushed a kitchen chair over to the sink, climbed up the chair and into the basin, and turned the water on. He found the spray gun and laughed and laughed as he squirted water all over the room. He did this, or attempted to do this trick, repeatedly. If I wasn't watching or listening for the sound of the chair legs scrape across the linoleum, I was destined to get soaked.

During this time, I noticed Jack's language was not developing as expected. Other children his age spoke clearer and were able to articulate their needs. Jack became frustrated. He would point, physically push to direct me to something he wanted, or he would get one of his brothers to decipher his needs, and they would do it for him. A few months later, when my, "he's the fourth child," excuse no longer seemed to hold water, I decided to take him in for a speech and language evaluation. He was diagnosed with a receptive and expressive language delay and he began weekly therapy at their local rehabilitation hospital for children. Luckily, our insurance covered the bulk of the cost, and it was right in our hometown.

In light of Jack's progress in speech therapy, Jack began attending a local preschool program and although he seemed to like his new school and teachers, he had difficulty during drop-offs. His teacher noted that during transitional times, when he was moving from one activity to another, Jack was slow to join and on occasion he flat out refused. He played next to his class-mates, as he had done at train table at the children's museum, but never with them. The teacher reported he appeared to have an awareness of the other kids, but he rarely engaged or played with them. I told myself it would get better and that once he got into a routine he would adjust to his new preschool and make friends.

Later that fall, we noticed Jack "zoning out," especially if the television was on or if he was playing with a favorite toy. We called his name several times and no response. He eventually came-to, but it was worrisome. It wasn't typical behavior for his age. The speech pathologist thought that this could be a processing glitch, which would fall under the category of his receptive speech delay. To cover all the bases, we scheduled a hearing evaluation. Thankfully, the test results reflected Jack had full range of hearing.

As we entered January of 2008, we left the chaos of the holi-days behind and the boys got back into the routines of school and scheduled activities. This was harder for Jack. He dragged his feet when prompted to get ready for school. Some days were better than others. Bribery worked in the beginning, and I allowed him to take his favorite train to school. This backfired when he took his beloved Henry the steam engine into class and another child attempted to grab it. Jack shoved him and ran away. Jack did not understand the school rule that any toy brought in was to be shared. Fat chance. We decided Henry had to stay in the car, but this was not sunshine and cupcakes either. As soon as I unbelted his car seat in the school parking lot, he melted down. He kicked, yelled, and huge crocodile tears ensued. He was fixated on bringing in his train.

Initially, I passed it off as being strong-willed and stubborn. God knows we had a few in our family; the kid was genetically inclined. But, why was this so hard? At times I got angry and raised my voice. This didn't help. Was it because he was the "baby" and I let things slide with him sometimes? Was I paying for being too soft and laid back? Maybe. But it felt like something more. I decided to call the public-school district and spoke to a special educator about my concerns.

After the speech and language pathologist observed Jack, she recommended further testing. I filed my request for several educational evaluations and was told it would happen within forty-five school days. It felt like forever. What if it was autism? Or something else? My two oldest children were both diagnosed with ADHD, but Jack presented differently. I knew early intervention was paramount and could feel time ticking way as we anticipated the results.

The public-school testing confirmed what had been reported in the speech and language evaluation. The school psychologist conducted an evaluation using the Differential Assessment of

Autism and other Developmental Disorders (DAADD). Nothing was clearly flushed out during the testing as his percentages were not high enough to secure a diagnosis, but it was noted that a behavior plan would be beneficial for him in the future. During the reading of his report at the IEP meeting, the psychologist used the example of Pavlov's dogs in regard to my son. I remember feeling both amused at his unprofessionalism and offended. After the IEP meeting, no one from the school moved forward in creating any type of behavior plan for Jack. It was like the meeting never happened. As the weight of the files lay heavily on my mind, I wondered if, at the age of three, a behavior plan had been enacted, would it have made a difference?

I thumbed through the file box and my fingers landed onto a folder marked, *testing*. I pulled the thick file out from the case and brought into my chest and closed my eyes. I heard the hum of the refrigerator in the kitchen and Jack's audio book playing down the hall.

Jack's symptoms persisted and I continued to probe for answers. I asked our pediatrician for help, and after hearing my concerns, he recommended a neurologist from Massachusetts General Hospital who worked a couple days a week at the local rehabilitation hospital where Jack was getting his speech therapy. Because the neurologist had begun seeing patients only recently, I had a good chance to have Jack seen in short time, bypassing a lengthy waitlist that existed at the hospitals in Boston.

Jack was scheduled to see the neurologist in February. As requested, I filled out the developmental paperwork and was prepared with a two-page narrative of observations and what our concerns were. What I did not understand was that the appointment with the neurologist was a screening, not an evaluation.

There was no hard data taken, nothing graphed or compiled other than observations from his preschool teacher and me, his mother. In my ignorance, I did not understand that a *screening*, especially for someone high functioning, is ill equipped to provide enough information to create a complete picture of our son. The neurologist determined that in addition to continuation of speech and language therapy, he would benefit from attending the public integrated preschool program. He noted Jack's profile suggested he may have a future prognosis of Attention Deficit Hyperactivity Disorder but did not diagnose him with ADHD at this time.

During Jack's Kindergarten year, we had a full neuropsychological evaluation done on Jack by a local private party. The neuropsychologist diagnosed Jack with ADHD. I was not surprised by the diagnosis, but I still could not shake the feeling that a missing piece remained. Maybe I was overreacting… maybe it was just a severe case of ADHD?

Mike and I requested an occupational therapy evaluation, specifically to address the dexterity and lack of control observed in his handwriting. As his teacher noted, he also had difficulty in reigning in his body during school hours, particularly during transitional times in their schedules. When children were walking in-line from the classroom to an activity, Jack wouldn't find his pacing. He either was too far behind or too close to the child in front of him. Sometimes he'd stop altogether. She also reported he spun in class. If he was moving from one area of the classroom to another, instead of walking he spun towards his desired location. With the feedback from his Kindergarten teacher, we requested the school test him for any sensory processing issues. In addition to the school's evaluation, we piggy-backed it with testing done by a private facility. The school's criteria differed from that of a medical institution's criteria, and by getting two different evaluations, the truth would lie in the middle. After the OT results came back, he was diagnosed with Sensory Processing Disorder (SPD) as well as dyspraxia. The diagnosis of dyspraxia explained Jack's underdeveloped fine motor skills as well as his difficulty in the area of large motor planning. It took more time for Jack to learn how to catch a ball than it did his brothers or peers. These delays in motor planning often manifested a high level of frustration, particularly in writing. Jack had big ideas and a vivid imagination, but to put them all down on paper as fast as he was dreaming them inside him mind was an impossible task.

By the end of Kindergarten, Jack had collected several diagnoses. As we sat at around the table during his annual Individual Educational Plan (IEP) meeting, we noted his newest diagnosis of SPD and dyspraxia. It was at this meeting, where Jack's kindergarten teacher spoke up candidly about his need for therapeutic support structured within the school day. Jack had begun his special education journey with a language delay and had made great strides in areas of his speech and language goals, but it was clear that he was lagging behind in his letter sounds and reading skills. It was recommended that Jack would benefit from the reading support program, Title One, in first grade. Occupational Therapy (OT) services were added into the framework of Jack's IEP, after his teacher said she didn't feel comfortable leaving the meeting without it being addressed and added to his educational programming. Jack would have access to the sensory gym and be taught strategies for self-regulation. Writing goals were added to assist in strengthening his hand muscles and motor control. Even though Jack received OT services in school twice a week, it was only for a half hour. We accessed our health insurance plan and Jack began to work with an OT weekly, in an outside therapeutic setting at the same institution where he was evaluated.

In November of 2011, Jack began to refuse to do his homework. Although I knew pen and paper tasks were hard for him, I offered breaks and reinforced our family rule of "work before play," which all the boys knew meant homework and chores before video games. Although this strategy got traction, I called a meeting with his school team and we met in early December. Neither his first-grade teacher, nor his support staff, had seen work refusal in the classroom. Around the same time, Mike and I noticed a decline in Jack's attention span, and we took the advice of his pediatrician and placed him on an ADHD medication. By February, he had escaped from school twice and his frustration level was climbing by the minute. Mike was able to slide him into an appointment with a neurologist, as we were concerned with Jack's uptick in behavior. The doctor recommended he be taken off of the ADHD stimulant and placed on Prozac to stabilize his mood. He diagnosed Jack with anxiety and depression.

As I snapped the file box lid, I thought about the paper trail we had collected over the past several years. I'd like to say I felt hopeful that we had screenings and reports, but I didn't. I was afraid. We had acquired all of this—a whole file box of information, and it still didn't capture the true nature of his deficit. What would we find next? Would it be another piece to the puzzle? Or would we have our answer? I remember my resistance to the labels, particularly with my first two children, both diagnosed with ADHD. Mike and I struggled with them having the weight of a term defining them, potentially limiting them in the eyes of others. As my oldest son began to fall apart in third grade, we decided to take the medication route. Using medication was never an avenue I wanted, but it was a tool for them to access during school hours. The noise and level of distractions in a school setting were challenging and it was easy for both Patrick and Kieran to become overwhelmed and lost during instruction. Other tools were implemented over the years, but maybe if I let go of my perceived notion that labeling would limit my children, I would've been open to other ways they could have accessed support. And let's face it, none of Jack's older siblings were running from the school with a trail of injured and bewildered staff behind them. Their struggles were quieter.

I shook my head as I felt a twinge of guilt. I didn't have the capacity to sit in session with the "itty-bitty-shitty-committee" today, the metaphorical group inside my head that told me all the ways I could've done things differently with my kids. The negative banter of "if onlys," or "what ifs," or my favorite, "I should have…," internal dialogs that fill my head, are something most mothers have.

4

SPIDERMAN

*a*s Mike and I stood waiting in the foyer of the school, I glanced around and took in the bright and colorful still-life sketches plastered on the walls in the entryway. Two male figures were standing a short way down the corridor, in front of the conference room with their backs turned toward us. Jack's special educator, who was the contact person on his IEP, walked down the same hall and paused at the two men. She motioned at her watch and continued moving toward us. She greeted us and directed us to the conference room.

We followed her toward the room. As we got closer, I saw that it was the school social worker and Jack's injured aide that were lurking in front of the door. The aide's arm was in a sling, presumably from his elbow injury that Jack had caused, and the social worker's hand was bandaged in a splint. They were the walking wounded, the ones who were harmed by being in my son's path. Were they both coming into the meeting? I nodded my head as we walked past them into the room.

The conference room was small and clearly used for other purposes in a past life, possibly an office, but now it was a space where meetings were held, and old chairs and desks came to die. Interestingly enough, this was also the room where Jack would spend his time out of the classroom, where he would do his schoolwork. We took our seats at the far end of the large rectangular table that faced the door. Various professionals came in — the social worker, both the vice principal and principal, Jack's teacher, and the director of pupil services. Mike and I were seated at the far end of the table. Staff filed in around the rectangular table.

"First of all, I want to thank the parents for your support during this difficult time and meeting with us today. We appreciate your willingness to seek guidance from medical professionals and your ability to work cooperatively in past meetings. We have provided Jack with a highly trained ABA one-to-one aide and have tried different plans with him at the school," the principal began, her forced smile fading as she continued.

"We have come to a difficult spot. Jack has left school on three occasions and multiple staff members have been injured." She tilted her head toward the social worker, then leaned back slightly in her chair and glanced over to Mr. Rafferty, the head of pupil services.

"The school district would like to propose some changes to Jack's education plan. We would like to suggest he attend the Collaborative School for a 45-day period. They are equipped to make in-depth behavioral assessments that include treatment on site," Mr. Rafferty explained.

My mind tried to grasp his recommendation. I was unaware of having a collaborative program in our area.

"I spoke to the director at the Collaborative and she has a spot available for him. We would like you to meet with her and tour the school. You would need to sign a consent form, so that we can share information with the director about Jack and in the event that you agree to this placement, we can get things moving quickly."

Mr. Rafferty had a plan. He had a plan for a boy he didn't really know. Staff sat silent and still as if they were onlookers to a tennis match. Mr. Rafferty kept the focus on us and looked for a response. The repetitious thumping sound of a large copy machine collating papers was heard through the conference door. Mike cleared his throat.

"You failed. You failed to keep our son safe. You put into jeopardy our son's life and your staff members. They got hurt because of your incompetence to keep a little boy in your care," his voice was calm and controlled, calculated, and severe. In slow motion, I watched as his words slice through the principal. Her expression moved from horror to indignation.

"Mr. Donovan, I beg your pardon, we have done all that we can to educate your son," she exclaimed. The vice principal, who sat alongside her, also shared visible disbelief.

"You failed. My son was in danger because of your incompetence. You have not done your job. You have failed him."

My body stiffened. I brushed away the tears that were streaming down my face. I was afraid Mike would yell. I was afraid things were going to spin further out of control.

"We have done so much for your son. We tried our best to put things into place for him," the vice principal added quickly.

"Now, Mr. Donovan, I think we can all appreciate that this is a serious situation and that when things of this nature are discussed emotions are right at the surface," Rafferty interjected attempting to diffuse the situation. His eyes were like saucers, wide and round, and there was an alertness to his posture, a readiness to pounce…or possibly run. "We want to help Jack move to a place where he can be assessed, and treatment decisions can be made."

"I don't know who you think my son is. He was in your office, in your care and he ran out of the school and was caught by a complete stranger?" Mike said, looking directly at the vice principal. "The carnage that followed my son is unbelievable—a fractured elbow, chipped tooth, sprained wrist… The way you speak about him, how fast and strong he is, makes me envision Spiderman, not my 7-year-old first grader," he said. There was frustration in his voice. "My child is not Spiderman or superhuman. He does not intentionally hurt people. There is a reason why Jack ran. There is a reason why he acted the way he did." His voice leveled out, smooth and even.

I looked over at my husband, dressed in a shirt and tie, straight from work, his sheer bald head glistened slightly with perspiration from the lights above, and from the strain and stress.

"This is why we believe that the Collaborative School would be a better placement option for Jack at this time," Rafferty said, trying to reign in the conversation.

"What are the other options?" I asked.

"This is the only option on the table right now."

"So, you're saying that the collaborative program is the only placement option for Jack?" I asked.

"Yes, it's only a forty-five-day placement so they can assess him and put a treatment plan together. After the forty-five-day period, we will meet with the staff at the Collaborative, see how he is doing, and if he is ready to come back into the public school system."

"So, after forty-five days he can come back to Bradford?" Mike asked. "That brings us to the end of the school year."

"They also offer a summer program, so if he is not ready to return at that time, he could continue through the summer at the Collaborative, and return back into Bradford in the fall."

Mr. Rafferty's eyes shifted. He was lying. I didn't believe him. It wouldn't be 45 days.

"Currently, we have a student that is in the process of transitioning back into the district from the program at the Collaborative. He has come a long way and is doing beautifully." He continued to sell it.

"How long this student has been out of district? Was it more than forty-five days?" I asked.

"Well, that is a different case—a different child, but yes, it took a bit longer. But, again, we would like you to take a look at it and see if you feel it would be right for your son. If you are willing to meet with the director and tour the school, we would like to have you sign a release form—for communication purposes," he clarified once more.

"We would like a copy of Jack's discipline record," Mike responded.

"Ah, yeah, we can make a copy of that." Rafferty threw a concerned look over at the principal, as this would be her responsibility.

"Yes, we can make a copy of that for you." Her gaze moved from him to us.

"We will consider meeting with the Collaborative and signing a release form for communication. We need to take some time to digest all that has happened," Mike told everyone.

As we wrapped up the meeting, Mr. Rafferty told us that the district would be providing Jack with a tutor while decisions were being made. He jotted down the names of outside services that Jack was receiving and had questions about therapies and if he was on any medications. I told him that Jack had recently begun taking Prozac at the end of February. Rafferty wrote down the information and noted his new diagnoses of anxiety and depression.

There were no pleasantries upon the close of the meeting, just a sea of bodies making their way to the conference room door. It was unlike any other school meeting we had attended before. It was draining and utterly unsatisfying, but it was over. We knew what they were proposing. Now, we just had to figure out what we wanted for Jack.

5

SCHOOLED

*A*fter a few rounds of phone tag, Mallory gave me Jane's contact information. Jane Sterling had been her son's educational advocate for years. Jane was in tune with the Burbridge Public School system, advocating for many families, as well as her own kids. Although we were a bit unsure if this was the direction we wanted to go, we made an appointment for a consultation. If nothing else, it would provide information to aid us in our decisions moving forward. Hiring a lawyer was not off the table. If we decided to go in that direction, we were confident Jane could give us some names.

We farmed the kids out for playdates to friend's homes so we could talk unhindered by small ears or tender hearts. Jack was still reeling from leaving school, the trauma of the event bringing about this current state of limbo and uncertainty. I needed to make sure that we had a solid plan before we introduced it to him.

We met Jane, on Sunday afternoon. We gathered around the dining room table; she removed her steno notebook from her briefcase and uncapped her pen.

"First of all, tell me, how is Jack doing?"

"He is okay, but it's been a hard few days. Emotionally, we all feel a bit raw," I responded, reading the concern on her face.

"At the team meeting last week, you mentioned the district recommended a forty-five-day placement at the Collaborative program. After our conversation on the phone, the way you described Jack and the level of his cognitive abilities, I am unsure if this would be a proper placement for him. In light of that, you should both visit the facility, see the classroom he would be placed in, and meet with the director." Jane was searching my face for a reaction.

"I think she's right," Mike said. "We have no grounds to say that it's the right placement for Jack if we don't go and see it for ourselves. And even if it is, I am not sure how we would be able to pay for it."

"I just cannot believe that it is our *only* option. What happens if we say no? Where does Jack go then?" My voice trailed upward.

"They have to educate your son. It's the law," Jane said. "What they are trying to do is ship him out of district because they want to have someone else deal with the mess they have created. His behavior has escalated from refusing to do his schoolwork to clearing desks and escaping from the school. These behaviors were reinforced by how staff and administration handled his non-compliance. The act of removing him from class and calling you to get him from school reinforced his actions. If he acted out, he didn't have to complete his work. Their inability to proactively step in, to address where his behavior was stemming from, is why we are here."

Jane cleared her throat and continued, "And to address your concerns, Mike, about paying for the Collaborative, the district is obligated to educate Jack. This is a private school, one that specializes in servicing kids who need a more restricted and supportive environment. It would be an out-of-district placement, paid for by Burbridge."

"Did they ever do a Functional Behavioral Assessment on him? This would typically be done by the school's behaviorist." Jane asked, switching gears.

"No, not to my knowledge," I said looking at Mike. "They did have her observe Jack in his classroom and the teacher said that they started giving him positive reinforcements for when he completed expected tasks."

Jane explained that typically, they would conduct a Functional Behavioral Assessment (FBA), to pinpoint the origin of his behavior—to identify the antecedent prior to the maladaptive behavior. The data is collected for the FBA and targets specific areas. From the objective data, the behaviorist creates a Behavior Intervention Plan (BIP), a document of procedures and directives to be followed by staff to re-shape maladaptive actions to expected ones. The success of any solid plan is that it is firmly grounded in data, not thrown together by a couple of half-assed observations and teacher interviews. If they had created a BIP, we had never seen it.

"When did you notice a change in Jack's behavior?" Jane asked.

"In late November, he started refusing to do his homework —crying and carrying on. We wondered if it was too much and it was causing him stress. We requested a team meeting. At the time, they were not seeing any of these behaviors. He was doing his work in class (although the writing workshop was hard for him), going to OT twice a week and Reading Recovery each morning."

"And when did he escape from the school?" Jane questioned, jotting down notes on her pad.

The first time Jack escaped was in December shortly after that team meeting. He was waiting in the dismissal area of the cafeteria and walked out the side door. The second time was in January. He escaped mid-morning, walked out of the classroom, and out the exit doors at the end of the first-grade hallway. The teacher in the classroom next to his had noticed him walking away from the building through the playground outside her window. He was retrieved by staff and brought back inside.

We had another team meeting at the end of January, to discuss these elopements, and his recent refusal to complete assignments in class. After he returned to school from holiday break, he refused to complete his classwork, and hid in his coat cubby to avoid sessions with his reading teacher. Even on days she coaxed Jack out from behind his coat, when they got down to her classroom, he would sit there and not do a thing.

"It was at that meeting that they first mentioned the school behaviorist. She was to observe Jack in his classroom. They discussed formulating behavioral strategies and the possibility of moving him to a different first-grade classroom," I added.

"Why were they talking about moving him? That is not something they typically do mid-year," she asked.

"The idea was brought up due the dynamics in his current classroom. When Jack had acted out, refusing to do work, pushing things off of desks or by disobeying the teacher's requests, he brought attention to himself. The kids in his classroom had labeled him as a troublemaker. He had become a bit of a spectacle."

I had been told the school behaviorist did come into the classroom and observed Jack. I was not told when or given any report or an official behavior plan. I was told that they had added behavioral strategies and had assigned an aide to help him in the classroom after the school behaviorist's visit. Ironically, I had suggested one-to-one support at the January meeting after he escaped from his classroom that month. The district cited that they couldn't line that up for Jack as they would need to hire a staff person and his teacher added that she would "watch him like a hawk" to ensure it wouldn't happen again. But it did.

"EDUCATIONALLY, they have not done anything to put a behavior plan into place. It sounds as though some observations have been taken, and a few behavior modifications have been added, but not systematically. They have been putting out fires, but not treating the issue at the core," Jane looked at us with earnest eyes. "*Why* is he is acting out? What is the antecedent? There is a *reason* for Jack's behavior. The data from observations in his classroom environment will lead us to these answers," she paused. "There *is* a reason, and we will get to the bottom of this together," she reassured us.

"And where are we right now? What is his status with the

school? Is he considered suspended? Or is he expelled?" she asked, directing the question at Mike.

"That is one of the things we wanted to ask you about," Mike said. "There is no suspension end date listed on his discipline record that they gave us. So, does that mean, by our conversation of alternative placement to the Collaborative, that he is expelled?"

Jane explained that she did not think it was legal to have an open-ended suspension date on a school document and she would consult her legal contact. In the meantime, she asked for a copy of Jack's recent evaluations and current IEP to review. We agreed visiting the collaborative program was necessary to determine if it was the right fit for Jack, as well as to create a case for why it wasn't. We would contact the school and to set up a tour. To prepare for the visit, Jane gave us a list of questions to ask the director.

"Find out what classroom they are grouping him into. Would it be the behavioral classroom? Make sure you ask her about the ages of the children that will be in Jack's class, the student-teacher ratio, schedule, peer-to-peer interaction and if they are taught social skills daily," she paused, allowing me time to catch up, then continued.

"One of the most important questions would be, what are the cognitive abilities of the children who will be in his class? And how can they differ instruction to accommodate Jack's educational needs?" she glanced down at Jack's recent educational report.

"We are talking about a kid who is very bright. He needs to be given work that is challenging him," she said and looked at Mike as she pointed to a graph within the packet.

"Yes, he is a bright boy. We have always known that. I have often said that the engine works fine, it's just the transmission that is a little mixed up," he explained.

Jane smiled when she heard this, but it soon faded. Her eyes move slowly over to me, her brow tilting inward, she asked, "Has anyone ever mention that he may be on the autism spectrum to you?"

There it was—Autism Spectrum Disorder. The diagnosis that Jack didn't have but had checked off all boxes around it. I took her back to when we had him screened by a neurologist affiliated with Mass General Hospital and the results being that he could have ADHD like his older brothers, but felt he was too young to give that diagnosis yet. He was officially diagnosed in Kindergarten and I explained the current diagnoses of Sensory Processing, Dyspraxia, reading delay, depression, and anxiety.

Jack exhibited "fight or flight" behavior during school. This was a physiological reaction that occurred when he perceived he was in danger. When Jack was agitated and lashed out, he was in "fight," and when he was running away or avoiding school assignments, he was in a "flight" response. Jack's perceptions were magnified by his disabilities, which triggered this primal response. I told her that it had only been a few weeks since he'd begun the Prozac and we were still in the process of getting the levels in balance.

Jane placed her hands on her note pad and looked at us squarely. She explained that based on Jack's description and his current diagnoses, his behavior could stem from autism. Unfortunately, she'd seen many cases of children who were undiagnosed and passed along to behavioral programs, putting both the student and the program in an impossible state. The program would not be able to properly treat the issue as they were missing the diagnosis. The child wasn't getting his needs met and was surrounded by other kids who had emotional issues, which could exasperate the undiagnosed student, thus creating more behavioral issues.

I became increasingly uneasy as she spoke. Jane must have sensed my discomfort and shifted gears.

"Is he still getting OT services outside of school?"

"No, we stopped that in late December, thinking maybe a therapeutic break would be good due to his homework load and the stress it was causing him," I said.

"Okay, well I think I have enough information to begin, and once I have a copy of Jack's file, I'll be able to fine tune a plan going into the team meeting on Wednesday," she said.

Mike and I agreed to call the school and plan a visit to the Collaborative program. As we walked Jane to the front door, she turned to face us. "I know this is not an easy spot you're in. But I want to tell you that your son will be okay, and I will do all that I can to make sure that he is given all that he deserves. Just hang in there."

THE NEXT DAY I made the dreaded phone call. I called Donna, the director of the Montessori preschool program I was working at and gave my notice. Even though I knew she and the owner would understand, I was devastated. I loved my students and felt at home within the walls of their homey school environment. I was in my second year at the preschool and it was my first job since I closed my home daycare business. Jack was just a baby then. Being back in the classroom and working with others who genuinely cared about children had given me confidence and a place stretch my creative wings. It was a loss to leave my position without saying a proper good-bye to the kids I served, but it was necessary. There was nothing I could have done about that. It was clear where I needed to be, at home with Jack. And Donna assured me, the door was always open.

6

SUSPENDED

We met Jane, our newly hired educational advocate, outside of the Bradford school a few minutes before our scheduled team meeting. After a simple greeting, we went inside, the three of us huddled into a corner of the lobby. My mind raced. Questions driven by trauma and fueled by fear were on a continuous loop inside my head. I looked at Jane hoping she would put my mind at ease.

"Thanks for delivering Jack's file. It was helpful. But, before we go into the meeting, I need to ask, how was your visit to the Collaborative?"

We had met with the director of the program the day before. She gave us a tour of the private program, the recommended placement for Jack. The school was nice and so were the people we met. The director was candid with us when speaking about the program, the length of time children typically stayed, and the role the district plays once a child was placed. Most likely, if Jack was placed there, it would be a year at a minimum. For most kids it was two years. Assessment and transition into the program took several weeks, maybe months. After that process, then the therapeutic work began.

In addition to the time, the director said that they very rarely had interactions with professionals from the district, unless it was during the admission process, or when students were transitioning back. We were able to observe the Emotional/Behavioral classroom. There were six kids and they were not doing much work at the time. The teacher explained that they were going to lunch shortly and that is why they were coloring and drawing. That being said, our observations of their interactions shed light on the cognition and level of behavior of these peers.

"Both Nicole and I feel like it would not be the right placement," said Mike.

I nodded in agreement as Jane glanced in my direction.

"I agree. After reading through Jack's latest test scores, and given the circumstances of his elopement from school, I feel that it could be more harmful than helpful for him," said Jane.

A breeze blew through the lobby and Robin, Jack's therapeutic counselor, came through the door.

"Your visit and thoughts on this placement will be questioned at this meeting. Mr. Rafferty will be chomping at the bit to place him. Having a child that is not being educated is not looked on kindly by the state. He will want to get this kid settled and accounted for as soon as possible."

"He has called us several times since Jack escaped from school, checking in and confirming our appointment with the Collaborative. *Very accommodating.*" Mike's sarcasm seeped out from under his pressed shirt and silk tie. Mike, who had fielded most of the correspondences with Mr. Rafferty since Jack's most recent escape, was bitter. He was bitter about how Jack was mishandled not only when he was in the school building, but now, too. Mike felt pressured by the district, which made us both angry. Where was this sense of urgency when Jack was refusing to do his homework, hiding under his desk in his classroom and running from the building?

"I am sure he has been," Jane responded.

Robin arrived in our circle smiling and greeted Jane as if they had met before. I knew that Jane had been an advocate for a long time, so this didn't surprise me. Robin knew of our experience of visiting the Collaborative and she also was not convinced that it was the ideal place for Jack.

Robin, a licensed Mental Health Counselor, had been working with Jack over the past several months to treat his ADHD. Robin specialized in teaching children how to gain control over ADHD symptoms through art therapy and other modalities. Our older son, who was diagnosed with severe ADHD, had received therapy from Robin and marked improvements were seen at home and school. We felt that Robin's expertise in ADHD, as well as her gentle nature, would help Jack as well. He began his therapy sessions in December shortly after our team meeting and Jack's homework strike.

We assembled around the rectangular conference table, once again in the cramped makeshift meeting room, and I noticed our meeting's guest list had expanded. The regular players were represented: the school principal, vice principal, social worker, special educator, and Jack's teacher. Additions to the meeting were the school behaviorist, Mrs. Booth, and our two new team members, Jane and Robin, of which the district was not notified that they would be attending on Jack's behalf. Maybe, it was one of the reasons why tension was palpable or maybe it was because they remembered when we were gathered six days ago, that Mike, in no uncertain terms, told them they had failed? Or maybe it was because one of their students vehemently hated being in their care and showed it by running from their building?

"Good afternoon. I know we have a lot of ground to cover, so let's begin." The school behaviorist, Jennifer Booth, cleared her throat and passed out two packets—the first one a summary of observations and the second one a Behavior Intervention Plan (BIP).

"I was able to observe on two occasions last month. On the first date, Jack had several incidences where he refused to comply with the end-of-the-day routines, such as retrieving papers from his cubby and packing up his backpack. He also was seen walking around the classroom, humming and singing to himself while the other children were either sitting at their desks or cleaning up."

Ugh. He had done this at home too. He would talk to himself, and in a sing-song tone he would review his day while in bed at night. He had done this for as long as I can remember. I'd recently mentioned this to Mike, pointing out the pitch of his voice, the inflections, and the way he talked to himself; I thought he would have grown out of it. I don't know if he was doing more lately due to stress, or if I just noticed it because he was seven, older than most kids who jibber-jabber.

"During the second visit, I observed him during writer's workshop. I was able to see more of the same non-compliant and refusal behaviors exhibited. During this work period, Jack's overall compliance with staff member's first requests was 33 percent of the opportunities presented. Just to give you an idea, we are looking to see 75 percent to 80 percent here," she said, looking up at Mike and me, realizing we probably didn't understand what that meant. I was grateful for the explanation, but it felt like another blow.

"During the spelling test, Jack refused to write down one word. His one-to-one aide, along with his teacher, periodically attempted to coax him to write the words. Jack still refused, and then appeared frustrated when other children were looking at him. He told one child sternly to not look at him. When that child didn't comply, Jack tossed a folder toward him."

"This pattern continued throughout the morning: redirection, refusal and non-compliance. Later, he had been working on the floor with his teacher using a moveable alphabet to create his spelling words; he struggled to spell the words and became frustrated. He ran across the room and barricaded himself in a corner surrounding his body with six chairs and a trash can. When the teacher told him that this was not safe and moved the chairs away, Jack walked over to the cubby area where he remained for several minutes without staff attention. After that, he did return to his desk unprompted, but when asked to do work, he slid under the table. Jack refused to come out using audible verbal refusals that included inappropriate language."

Mrs. Booth recommended the development and implementation of an individualized Behavioral Intervention Plan. She also recommended a social skills assessment, noting he had difficulty understanding the perspective of others.

We moved onto the Behavior Intervention Plan. At the top, the date read March 28, 2012. Yesterday. She pulled this together *after* he left! The familiar disbelief and frustration filled me. The report should have been titled "damage control" as it would've been more accurate.

I glanced over at Jane. She saw it too, right?

I flipped through the five-page document. There were four sections, each identifying an area of behavior targeted as problematic: refusal, aggression, escaping, and destruction. Mrs. Booth read through each section, noting what she perceived as the function of the behavior, either attention-seeking or avoidance/escape and what the antecedents were for these acts. Although her voice was clear and concise as she read the report, I caught her words and sentences in scattered installments, filling the margins with notes as I underlined key phrases and language I didn't understand.

"I cannot stress enough that this behavior plan is to be carried out with the highest level of consistency. If Jack escapes, for instance, after he is contained and demonstrates safe behavior, he needs to return or complete the task prior to his elopement. Jack needs to comply with what is expected of him. This is to be executed across the board."

Scanning the document, I read words like extinction, non-reinforcement, physically dismantling, discrete trials and the phase "waiting him out." There were descriptions and directives laid out for his teacher and aide to follow.

"How was this behavior plan created? Did you do a functional assessment on Jack?" Jane probed.

"I created the BIP from the observations as well as several interviews with his teachers and Jack's aide."

"So, there was no formal FBA completed? Having a Functional Behavior Assessment is key to be able to put a behavioral plan into place. We have seen that when academic demands are placed on him, he feels pressure and he bucks. Could we have a reduced schedule for Jack, allowing him to come back into school and have a proper Functional Behavior Assessment completed?" Jane asked as she shifted her eyes back to Mr. Rafferty, the school principal.

"With all that you have read to us, the way that this plan is to be followed, is this something that can be done here in our school setting?" Rafferty asked.

"In all honesty, no. I don't see how this plan can be followed in this active public-school environment," Mrs. Booth responded.

"Mrs. Booth, as our school behaviorist, would you be in support of Jack going to the Collaborative? Do you think he could be assessed there and placed on an effective program?" Rafferty pressed.

"Yes, I do. They have more areas and trained staff that can help in following a plan like this one."

Mr. Rafferty looked toward us. "I did have a chance to speak with the director of the Collaborative and she said that you folks came in for a tour the other day. What are your thoughts?"

"We did visit and were able to observe in Jack's intended classroom. After speaking with the director and seeing the class, I have to say that we feel that those children are more profoundly affected than Jack. Neither Nicole nor I can see Jack being a good fit for that program." Mike spoke confidently, looking squarely at Mr. Rafferty.

"Do we have a diagnosis yet?" Rafferty asked, now looking at me.

"Yes, he has been diagnosed with Attention Deficit Hyperactivity Disorder, Sensory Processing Disorder, anxiety and depression. He has recently started taking Prozac to help his mood disorder, but it will take time for it to build up in his system. I believe we mentioned this last week."

"And what about his ADHD?"

"His ADHD is being treated in my office," Robin responded.

"Without medication," the social worker pointed out.

"As I said—his ADHD is being treated in my office. I am helping him enlist tools and strategies to help him in this area," Robin glared at the social worker.

I understood why she glared at him. In my experience, as well as the feedback received by friends who had children similar to mine, teachers and administrators had mentioned the use of medication to help support children affected by ADHD. Was it because these educators couldn't "think outside of the box" for these active and gifted-minded thinkers? Or was it because they are not pigeon-holed learners? Was it likely that the teachers had too many kids and too little time to be able to accommodate all of the learning styles they were assigned to? I was not opposed to accessing all the tools that would help my child, but I was opposed to the idea that medication was the *only* way. It is only one tool in a box of many.

The meeting went on and on—different professionals sharing their professional opinions. The vice principal took us through a play-by-play of her experiences with Jack's escalation from Christmas break to the present moment. She was concerned that his level of aggression had become more and more elevated. The behaviorist stated a few of the components of BIP had been put into place prior to his last escape. Jane rebutted and stated the effectiveness of the plan could not be measured until everyone was on the same page. The principal chimed in, concerned for the safety of the children in Jack's class. The social worker was concerned for Jack's safety.

"We have seen Jack's behaviors escalate and when we put more controls in place, I am nervous that the staff will not be able to handle the extinction burst once the full BIP is implemented," the behaviorist pleaded with compassion in her eyes. "His behavior will get likely get worse before it gets better," she added. Extinction burst. I vaguely remember hearing this term in a college psychology class. The jargon used in the Behavior Intervention Plan and in the meeting sounded clinical. *Extinction burst?* He was a child who needed support, not a science experiment!

"If we thought we could do it here, we would. We do not commonly recommend out of district placement; only if we feel it is absolutely necessary." Rafferty followed up.

"If we intermittently reinforce the behavior plan, he will continue to exhibit behaviors. I am concerned about the variables that occur in a public-school setting. He will best be served in a therapeutic setting that can assess him and put a behavior plan into place and I believe that the Collaborative can do what we cannot at this time," added Mrs. Booth.

I was beside myself. They were insistent on this one program for Jack. They were recommending a behavioral/emotional program for a child whom they under assessed. And Rafferty... Had he even visited the program he was desperately recommending?

"We appreciate all your concerns. Nicole and I need time to digest the information presented today to get a clearer picture of what would be the best placement for our son," Mike said.

We wrapped the meeting up, and Mr. Rafferty mentioned

that he would look into securing tutoring services for Jack while we decided on placement. He would be calling us with the name of the tutor, and we requested that Mrs. Booth brief the tutor on Jack prior to meeting him. She agreed.

And that was that. No other mention of options for Jack's education, just the Collaborative and the promise of a tutor's phone number. The meeting was over and instead of leaving with a sense of relief, I felt drained and disheartened.

7

MISUNDERSTOOD

We met the district appointed tutor at a local restaurant on a weekday evening and grabbed a booth facing the door. A woman walked in and paused to speak to the hostess. The girl pointed towards us. The woman nodded and with heavy hurried steps she headed our way. She apologized for being late before she even reached the table.

We ordered drinks, allowing her a minute to catch her breath and time for me to mentally review the list of questions that Jane and I went over earlier that day.

"Thank you for meeting us. I know that this extends your workday," Mike offered kindly. He explained the intention of our meeting was to determine if she and Jack would be a good match. She cocked her head slightly as if she hadn't realized it was that kind of meeting.

"Let me start by asking you, what is your experience in working with children?" Mike asked.

She summarized her work history, which entailed tutoring children who had been out of school due to long-term illnesses. Although it was clear that she loved kids, she did not have background in special education, or any noted behavioral training.

"I spoke to Mr. Rafferty briefly and he told me that this would be a temporary assignment, just until placement has been decided. He approved two hours a day, five days a week for Jack. He mentioned that Jack was having a hard time staying in school," she wrung her hands over the table in front of her.

Well, that was an understatement! Having a hard time staying in school? Did he mention that he hits, kicks, and runs out double doors making staff members chase after him? Did he explain to you that Jack was really a superhero in a pint-sized body? How incredibly fast and skilled he was? How he can execute an escape that even Houdini himself would be impressed by? I thought.

"Well, that is true. Jack does have difficulty staying in school, at times he refuses to complete his classroom work and has become combative," Mike replied.

"What would you do if Jack refuses to do his work? How would you handle it?" I asked, taking my cue as this was on my list of questions.

"If it came to it, I would just wait him out. In the past, I have used a reward system that has worked well with many of my clients," she said.

"And if he ran?" Mike asked her.

"Well, has he ever run from the home setting before? I was under the impression that he only ran from school?" she looked perplexed.

"Yes, he has only run from the school, but if we are placing academics into the home setting and this historically has set him off, our feeling is that we may see these behaviors return." I watched her shift in her padded seat, her eyes moved around as if she was mulling over the information, formulating her next move, but came up empty.

"Oh," she said.

After we tossed out a few more questions, it was apparent that there was a communication gap between the district and the tutor. It made me question how much thought and effort went into choosing this woman for this job. Did Mr. Rafferty take into consideration the behavioral challenges that were descriptively laid out in the last few meetings? How this young boy needed to be in a specialized setting due to his behavioral and emotional needs? And they send us her? Not only was she unqualified, she appeared to get winded rushing over to our table. One can only imagine her trying to chase after Jack…

After our meeting ended, we lingered in the booth alone and finished our coffees, both of us frustrated and angry, me more than Mike. I think he understood the strategic planning—the hoops that one has to go through—to get to the next level. Was it negligence? Or was it strategically planned so that we would opt for the collaborative program they pushed? My brain hurt, and so did my heart.

We brainstormed other programs in the area, one being a Montessori school. They were private and might be a good fit for a kid like Jack. Unfortunately, the Montessori school, as with the other ideas we floated around, was not equipped to deal with Jack's behavioral side or the level of supports he needed, an IEP with occupational therapy and reading services. At this point, we suspected there could be additional diagnoses that would get teased out over time, so that was another concern about private schools and limited resources. Unless the school was geared toward special needs, the therapeutic support was not there.

We were back to the collaborative program which, again, was not academically the right fit. And we had concerns about the high level of emotional and behavioral needs of current students, what their backgrounds (traumas) were, and how that would impact Jack. Would the behaviors of others exasperate him, possibly adding additional emotional strain to a boy who was already exhibiting an acute response to stress? Moreover, we believed Jack was being placed into the wrong classroom.

I had entertained the idea of homeschooling as an option. There was a wonderful local network of families who had chosen this educational option. I contacted a homeschooling mom and she explained what she did with her kids and how they met with other homeschoolers for socializing and educational outings. But the reality was, if Jack's behaviors revved up, I wouldn't have support or knowledge at home to deal with it. Homeschooling also felt like a long-term commitment, and without the supports —therapeutic and otherwise—I would be putting myself in a tough position. I didn't feel confident that I could take on the additional roles and meet Jack's needs. The behavioral intervention, planning, and teaching an educational curriculum, as well as understanding his IEP and how to access these tools for him was a lot to deliver.

Mike believed the school needed to be accountable for educating Jack. Both of us struggled with the labels Jack had collected over the past several years, not because it made him less, but because the labels could be limiting. We learned, however, that the educational system required labels (diagnoses) to secure supports, so we pursued getting evaluations and pressed forward in areas where Jack was falling behind. Our conversation went around and around until we finally returned to where we started. It was hard to sit and wait, to gather more facts, but it was necessary. We did not have all the information we needed, as parents or educators, to place him in a program—yet.

THE DAYS RAN INTO WEEKS. We were waiting to hear back from Jane about a tutoring company she suggested to Mr. Rafferty that specialized in children with educational and behavioral challenges. He said he would look into it and get back to us. Tick-tock. Tick-tock. Tick-tock. It was becoming increasingly difficult not to take this whole mess personally, particularly since the tutor he assigned was unqualified. Prior to our rejection of recommended school and tutor he was all over us with phone calls and emails.

My head was like a three-ring circus on a continuous loop of thoughts that jumped from ring to ring, making it hard to focus. Jack rolled in. He did it often—he rolled from room to room as a mode of transportation. I think that it stems from his need for sensory stimulation.

"Mom…mom…MOM!" I finally tuned into Jack's request for attention.

"Oh, yes Jack, so sorry honey. What can I do for you?" I looked at him as he stayed in the tucked position, balancing on his bottom, while he tried not to fall over.

"Well, Mom, I was wondering if I...could...play the...Wii?" he sputtered out, struggling to keep his balance.

"We finished lunch a little bit ago and you did work on your math facts, so I think we should go to the playground for a few minutes before we pick up Aidan at school," I said as I watched him lose his fight for stability. His unraveled body laid flat on the carpet. With his arms and legs extended, he mimicked his best starfish.

"Ugh...are you SERIOUS?! I did my work, can I just play for a little while before we go?" his limbs tightened, his brow knitted.

"You know that this is during school hours and you cannot play the Wii during school hours, but you can play a game or Legos, until it's time to leave."

"That's so unfair! Why can't I play the Wii? I have done ALL my work. It's not fair!" He was sprawled out in front of me on the floor, his hands now clenched into fists, beating them onto the rug.

"I know you want to play the Wii, and you will, after we have our outside time. It is part of our routine, just like when you have recess at school."

"But I don't HAVE recess anymore, Mother. I don't even have school!"

"Well, if you want your Wii time, you know what you need to do," I said, directing my attention away from him to the unfolded basket of laundry.

"Fine!" he said, in a huffy tone, folding himself up again and rolling out of the room. A few minutes later, I heard a familiar click...the television turned on. It was not technically the Wii, but it wasn't one of the suggested activities. I finished folding the laundry, took a deep breath and headed into the living room. As the show's credits began to roll, I grabbed the remote and turned off the television.

"Okay Jack, you have a choice, you can play in our yard or on the playground at the school?" I said, hoping he would not see through my plan of getting him outdoors.

"I'll go to the playground. But I'll get time on my Wii when I get home, right, Mother?"

This whole "Mother" thing was new. He seemed to go back and forth between calling me Mom and Mother.

"Yes, Jack. You've earned your video game time."

"YES!" he shouted and bolted out of the room.

I WALKED INTO THE CAFETERIA, which was a mob scene even on a good day. Parents waited by the entrance or on the opposite end of the room by the stage. There was usually one over-stimulated teacher's aide waiting to sign people out. I lined up with the other parents who stood against the wall and waited. Jack begged me to let him stay on at the playground. I can't say I blamed him. It was loud and chaotic inside. Kids ran about while moms chatted with each other. As my eyes scanned the room, I noticed a couple of women by the stage. One of them was a mom from Jack's former first-grade class, the one he escaped from. She was looking over at me and talking to a taller woman with long black hair who turned in my direction. After we made eye contact, they twisted away, their heads leaned in closer to finish whatever point the blond one was making. Were they talking about me? As if she heard me, the black-haired woman stole another glance in my direction.

More kids scurried into the large room. I spotted Aidan with a friend chatting away. I noticed he was considerably smaller than his friend, another boy in the third grade. His brown hair appeared lighter, catching the rays of sunlight that streamed in from the enormous windows.

"Hi Mom!" he said exuberantly. He had a great big smile on his face. I'd started to pick him up from school a few weeks ago. He had been bombarded with questions during his bus ride home, all questions about Jack... What happened to your brother? Did he really run away from school? Did he get expelled? Did you know he hit his teacher? Was he crazy? These were just a handful of inquiries that he would face on the twelve-minute bus ride home. Poor kid. He didn't really know how to answer them. He was caught in between trying to bridge the gap of being cool, loving his brother, and not entirely understanding why Jack did what he did either.

Aidan ran ahead through the cafeteria doors and sprinted down the path to the playground. It was early April and the air had started to warm. Daffodils stood proudly in clumps bursting under the crabapple trees that lined the playground area. I found the kids on the climbing structure. Jack was playing tag with a couple of boys. Aidan was scaling the ladder to reach the monkey bars. I located a bench and sat down. I closed my eyes and felt the sun on my face. The heat of the rays offset the cool sea breeze, keeping me humble.

I tuned into the noise of the playground banter. It was easy to discern which one was Jack. His was *always* the loudest. This was a helpful attribute while he played outside in our yard. I could hear where he was and what he was doing. I only really worried when it was quiet. Today was not a quiet day. The sound of kids running, racing, dodging, and chasing…Jack's loud boisterous voice was capping it all. He directed the kids where to go as they ran and climbed.

"Watch out!" he screamed. Jack was having a grand time, but when I opened my eyes, I saw the complete picture. The group of kids had dwindled down. Only two boys remained. Jack's movements were quick and jarring. His head snapped back and forth to track the "predator" who was chasing him. He moved with erratic gait, slightly uneven at times with his arms flailing. The way Jack moved through space was different than his peers. I couldn't help but wonder *if*, or *when*, his peers would notice.

One of the children pulled the other one aside and said something to him. I watched the way they gestured and pointed. It appeared they were leaving too. I wasn't surprised, as neither of them could get a word in, or position themselves without Jack shouting out orders… "No, don't go that way! I told you to go *around* the slide!" Was his desire to control this game his response to a life that had spun out of control? His self-regulation before he left school and since had been unpredictable. He was more sensitive to everything—sounds, situations, demands.

Neither did he recognize when his voice level raised or when he was beginning to get frustrated. In retrospect, Jack had never excelled in the area of self-awareness or self-regulation, but now there was no way of denying his struggles.

"Jack and Aidan! Come on boys, it's time to go home." I pulled the plug before Jack had a chance to notice the other boys had disengaged, my way of wrapping him up in invisible bubble wrap, trying to keep him protected from further disappointment.

It was becoming second nature to anticipate the actions of others or gauge Jack's reactions to situations. There was a palpable urgency to protect Jack during this delicate time, to make sure he was set up for success, not failure. This was one thing in all of this mess that I understood with certainty.

8

A BOY WITHOUT A HOME

Several weeks had passed since we rejected the district's recommendations for an alternative school placement and tutor. At home, I created a routine for Jack. Each day, we did some sort of educationally based outing, as well as reading and math facts. We spent time in Woods Hole at the fisheries aquarium, staring at the fish, lobsters, and sea creatures. We talked about scientists, marine biologists, and the different types of research that touched Cape Cod and the world. We went and toured the Mayflower in Plymouth, pretended we were pilgrims and imagined we were on the ship being tossed around at sea, what it was like to start a new life in a wild land. We walked through town and read monuments and talked more. We visited playgrounds, libraries, fishing harbors, and museums.

That was the teacher in me. The mother in me wanted to make sure that he was protected, by shielding off any comments like, "Shouldn't you be in school, young man?" by the elderly women standing in the check-out line of the post office. Jack responded curtly, telling her to mind her "own damn business," and I swiftly escorted him out of the building. Unintentionally, the woman had triggered his anxiety. Because of that interaction, we came up with strategies—scripts—of how to answer questions and inquires. At first, he would say, "I get homeschooled by my Mom," and once he began tutoring services, it changed to, "I get tutored at home." Having answers to this particular line of questions, which were asked frequently, lessened his uneasiness.

His medicine seemed to be working. His body appeared slightly less rigid and we had not seen any explosive meltdowns at home. He would bargain, sure, he always wanted to debate about getting more time with preferred activities. The reality was that our schedule did not take anywhere near the time it took for a regular school day. I allowed for electronics after his older brother came home from school, marking an end to his academic day. Although I was not homeschooling him (I had no curriculum, workbooks, etc.), I wanted to create a sense of order. It gave him space to regroup and reset. Time that he desperately needed.

Jane believed that Jack would benefit from an educational tutoring company who had expertise in the area of special education and behavior. Jane spoke to Caroline Chase, the owner of Atlas Educational Services, and a Board Certified Behavior Analyst (BCBA) who was known in her field for her high caliber work. Jane contacted the district on our behalf and recommended Atlas as Jack's educational service provider.

Other than looking at the Collaborative and meeting the ill-fitting tutor, no other options were presented, nor had educators from the school system contacted us. It had been a month-and-a-half. Our advocate was working behind the scenes to secure Atlas Educational Services, and we finally received news that it had been approved. Two weeks later, we were scheduled to meet Caroline.

The next thing was to contact Maggie Holden about occupational therapy and sensory integration services. As a part of Jack's IEP he received OT and PT at school, and the district was required by law to provide them regardless if he was attending school or not.

I had read a book on Sensory Processing Disorder called *The Out of Sync Child* by Carol Kranowitz and Lucy Jane Miller, which had helped me to identify some of Jack's symptoms prior to Jack's escape from school. I knew that he was out of sorts and had difficulty controlling his body. I remember watching him spin down the hallway while he was walking to the school bathroom. He pressed his body against the wall, leaned into it and rolled along...all the way to the boy's room.

I dialed the phone to schedule a consultation with the occupational therapist. At the very least, I figured I could leave a message if she was in treating a patient. The phone rang and rang. I expected the voicemail to pick up any second when a cheery woman answered.

Without warning, I spilled everything out to Maggie. She listened, then asked me questions in a kind and soothing voice, took down necessary information and told me that she was happy to work with Jack. My hand was shaking as I jotted down notes. She had worked with our school district before, so she was familiar with the logistics of payment and contracts. The tension I had been unknowingly holding inside me released a bit. I had underestimated how important it was to me to obtain these services for Jack. It was helpful having another piece of Jack's programming come into focus.

Momentum felt good, but it was not enough to keep the fears at bay. In the quiet spaces, when I was not "doing something," the chatter inside my head woke up. I could barely hear my inner voice as it became entangled with the information and messages I had been receiving from family and friends. I felt bombarded with suggestions and remedies to our situation...*Maybe you should put Jack on a gluten-free diet. Do you want to borrow my book? So-and-so used to be a school psychologist, but has since retired, but when I told her about your son, she said she would love to help you. Here is her number, give her a call... did you call her yet? You should really give her a call. Have you thought about signing him up for gymnastics? That could be good for him. What about sending him to a private school? Have you thought about taking red dye out of his diet? I saw an expert on Dr. Oz who talked about how some kids were highly affected by those additives...* It went on and on, all of them with good intentions. All of them loved Jack. None of it helped me. It only heightened my anxiety, pulling me in every direction. Each suggestion wrapped around me like a wild vine, paralyzing me.

Some days I felt myself sink down into a guarded place. The isolation that was built into our day was bittersweet, bringing me both solace and fear. A part of me was comforted that he was with me and I knew what he was doing at all times. I was in control. With that said, I had to take Jack to places where he would have social opportunities, which, most of the time, consisted of local playgrounds with kids far younger than him. When I did bring him to a playground after school hours seeking children his age, it was stressful.

I realized Jack's reputation had preceded him, and that my protective mommy bubble was not foolproof and could be infiltrated. On several occasions, I saw him being questioned by peers, looked at snidely by cute girls with pigtails, and teased by boys his age (presumably due to his past behavior at the school). I also saw other moms eyeballing him. I saw other mothers, ones that I had chatted on the soccer sidelines with, look uncomfortable around me. Conversations were awkward or surface level. Even when I was not isolated, I felt alone.

The recent term, "helicopter parenting," was not helping either. It only added to the misunderstanding and separation from other parents. They assumed I was overbearing or too controlling, not allowing my child to learn direct consequences. One of the downsides of Jack's disability is that it was hidden. He looked like a typical kid, but he wasn't. He needed social cues pointed out, as Jack didn't read body language. He didn't understand social subtleties that other kids knew organically such as facial movements and gestures.

On the playground, I could feel the vibes from the parents and the kids, as well as that of my own kid. While other parents chatted, a transparent cord extended from me to Jack. I was "on," tapped into his energy. Like a barometer I gauged where he was emotionally, at all times. I was ready to step in to decode a situation for him or pull the pin if he was becoming too pressurized.

The backlash of Jack's situation was affecting my two other children at the K-8th grade school they attended. Aidan, the third grader, was becoming irritated and separating himself from peers on the playground. After receiving calls from his teacher about his change in demeanor, we decided to seek help for him with an outside therapist. I had lost faith in the school for handling the sensitive nature of my children and had been picking him up daily from school since I found out he was being assaulted with questions about Jack on his bus. He was ill-equipped to navigate the curiosity and ignorance of his peers.

Jack was the talk of the school. Even before he escaped, his yelling, crying, hitting, and trips to the principal's office were well-known.

Kieran was in 7th grade. A few weeks after Jack's escape, I received an email from Kieran's math teacher, and instead of typing in his name, she wrote "Jack." But she never had Jack as a student—her daughter did. She must have gotten an earful about him from her daughter, who was Jack's teacher that year. The image of his name in black text was searing. Jack's story was *everywhere.*

We were all a bit tender and felt displaced in a community we called home. Like a pebble tossed into a pond, its impact disrupted the water and created energetic rings that expanded outward from the center. Nothing on the water's surface was spared from the disturbance. As the image played in my mind, I thought about the older boys. How the ripples affected them, individually and collectively. It was another concern, another worry, another thing to add to my pile of responsibility.

Once Jack started services, I would have more time to focus on the others. I felt guilty boxing it up and putting them aside for now, but it was only for another week. Or so I thought.

9

FIRST RESPONDERS

She stood in our living room and stared out of the large picture window while she watched my son walk away. Through the window I heard the wild inflection of his voice and could see his erratic hands dramatically tell his side of the story. His determined feet pounded the pavement as he turned left out of our driveway. I watched his new tutor with urgency. Was she going to go after him? Bring him back? What was her plan? Her lacquered mahogany mane was pulled back into a thick ponytail, while her eyes remained focused on him—the slowly disappearing young behavioral child who was in her care. Her weight shifted and she looked at her wristwatch, then over to me. She appeared athletically fit; if she needed to, she could take off and run after him, unlike the tutor the district originally assigned to him. This was consoling, but I still felt uneasy.

"Are you going after him?" Desperation broke through my voice.

"He'll come back," she said with a slight, but audible sigh.

"Well, how do you know? I mean what if he runs away or goes into my neighbor's garage and finds his power tools that he leaves out?" My pitch was pleading. I tried to collect myself.

"Let's wait a minute and see. He did great until the last few minutes and then he decided he was done. He is trying to avoid the work by escaping—leaving the house. Now, that we have been working with him in your home for a week or so, he realizes that we are here to have him do his schoolwork." She shifted and glanced down at her watch. "Although we are using a backdoor approach, there is an expectation to complete his daily assignments. He likes the science experiments—building volcanos and making them erupt, putting together robots with wires and batteries and measuring widths and heights of all sorts of objects— so he is learning, but through a backdoor. Today, we upped the demands in the area of his academics and his behavior spiked."

She gestured to the window.

"Shouldn't we go and get him?" Images of him in the garage with Jim's power tools were seared into my head. I rubbed my clammy hands onto my denim shorts.

"No, I see him. He is in the corner of the yard. See him in that tree?" She pointed. How could she be so blasé about this? Did we make a mistake in pushing for this educational company?

"Oh, okay, now I see him." He was sitting crouched on a branch, about ten feet off the ground.

"We are getting to know your son, learning what his triggers are, what behaviors he accesses in the home environment, so we can come up with a plan for him." She looked at me; her large blue eyes were soft and caring. "This is what we do, Mrs.

73

Donovan. It will be all right. We deal with kids like Jack all the time."

Jack had two educational tutors, Ainsley and Jill, who came on different days to work with Jack for two hours, five days a week. At first, Jack loved the attention, but when they increased demands, his behaviors gradually increased. He would cry, scream, run, and hide from his tutors. He hid in odd small places, like the corner cabinet on the kitchen counter, on a shelf in the linen closet under clean folded towels, or in his clothes hamper nestled in stacks of dirties. His tutors would wait him out, then have him complete the requested task that he was trying to avoid. Some days his tutor had to stay late to get compliance. This did not make him happy.

ANOTHER WEEK HAD PASSED, and I had gotten into the rhythm of our new routine. In the morning we usually got outside, either to a park or on a walk. After lunch, his tutoring session began. Jack and Ainsley were working in the dining room when I heard something smash and splinter against the wall. It sounded like the plastic container of sight-word craft sticks had been tossed. Silence. I sat frozen in a heap of clean laundry I was folding in the family room. I held my breath and waited.

"Jack, pick those up, so you can finish your work." Ainsley's voice was calm and even. Nothing. A few more seconds passed, then I heard the chair legs rumble against the floor, followed by pounding feet. Jack ran around the house, tipping over a basket of folded laundry, throwing books, tossing toys. He ran upstairs and hid in the closet. Ainsley followed him but kept a distance between them. After a few minutes, he leaped out and sprinted from the closet and back down the stairs. He ran by me in the foyer and into the kitchen, only pausing for a nanosecond to flip another basket of laundry. I waited for Ainsley at the bottom of the stairs. She walked past me, into the family room, then into the kitchen.

"See what you made me do?!" he yelled in a high-pitched voice. More silence.

"Jack, put down the knife," Ainsley directed.

What? Did she say *knife?*

"A little help, please?!" she shouted out the kitchen door. I came charging in, still processing the words. Jack was standing in front of Ainsley with a large chef's knife. He became distracted when I appeared in the doorway and Ainsley was able to grab the knife out of his hand. She reached over and handed me the knife, while Jack fell to the floor in a lump and started to sob. Stunned, I stood there with the large knife in hand, staring at the crumpled-up little boy on the floor. Ainsley took a couple steps back, glanced at her watch, then stared at the wall, waiting for Jack to pull it together. I turned and slid the knife back into the drawer then stood in front of it.

Over the next few minutes, Jack cleaned up the spilled sticks and finished reading his sight words in the dining room. "I-AM-DONE!" Jack shouted. He barreled out of the room into the family room. Sponge Bob's annoying laugh quickly jarred me from my post. After Ainsley finished packing up her materials, she walked over to me.

"Are you okay? I asked.

"Yes, I am fine. He is pulling out all the stops today."

"I am so sorry. I cannot believe he did that. He's never done that before—gotten *that* escalated."

A wave of thoughts crashed through my head. What if this was too much? What if they didn't want to keep working with Jack? What if they couldn't handle him—handle this? Were they going to tell the district? Would I have to send him away? I could feel my teeth chatter as nervous energy coursed through my body. I clenched down and tightened my jaw forcing them to stop.

"It's going to be okay. We just need to reassess and create a plan for him," she said with kind eyes. "I am going to talk to Caroline, and we will figure it out...I will see you tomorrow," she said and turned and walked out the door.

Ainsley contacted me the next morning explaining that she had spoken to Caroline and that they were meeting to come up with a plan for Jack. Afterward, a meeting would be set up with us to discuss the steps that would be implemented before the tutors came back to work with Jack. I was to tell Jack that Ainsley had the stomach bug, so he would not relate it to the knife incident that happened the day before. Caroline would reach out to us soon.

Suspended again. In mid-air we waited for the call.

A COUPLE OF DAYS LATER, we met with Caroline, Ainsley, and Jill. We arranged ourselves around the table. Caroline began. Her words were slow and deliberate as she summarized Jack's academics and his overall response to his work expectations. She paused and, although her tone had not changed, I felt a shift.

"There is something I wanted to discuss with you. Over the past several weeks that we have been working with Jack, we have seen his behaviors heighten and I feel as though something might be holding him back—neurologically. We have observed that Jack presents behaviors that are generally seen in children on the Autism Spectrum. When I was there, I noticed him bouncing his blanket—repeatedly—off of his chin. Jill has noted that he scripts," she said.

"Scripts?" Mike asked.

"He repeats lines from movies or television —but in his own world, like he is there, living in it," she explained.

My mind drifted to a place where I had seen this too… playing with his Legos or in the car or after I tucked him into bed. Scripting, as she called it, was Jack's personal soundtrack. I brought myself back to the words she had just said—Autism Spectrum Disorder.

"Having the neuropsychological evaluation with Dr. Chambers will be key. She will be able to tease out if it is ASD or whether she would characterize it differently, such as a nonverbal learning disorder. Having her test Jack will be more telling, but in light of what we have seen, I felt it was necessary to have this conversation with you, if only to prepare you." Caroline tilted her head; her warm hand touched my forearm. "Are you okay?"

"I always knew there was something wrong with Jack. With every new diagnosis, I kept thinking they didn't capture it all. At times I got the impression that people thought that I was on a witch hunt to find something that was not there. I felt alone, and at times, crazy." Pregnant with emotion, tears flowed freely down my cheeks.

"There is nothing *wrong* with your son. He is a bright and funny boy, who has a learning difference," Caroline reassured me. "There are so many kids like Jack. He is not alone…and neither are you." I took the tissue Jill handed me and dried my eyes.

"I think that Nicole and I are not totally surprised by this. It would explain so many things about Jack. Especially his behavior," Mike said, looking at me then to Caroline.

We had made an appointment for another neuropsychological evaluation after Jack escaped from school in March. The neurophysiologist came highly recommended as she had extensive experience with young children and adolescence. Caroline, who had worked with Dr. Chambers on other cases, said she would be happy to discuss the observations and data with her. They could also fill out any questionnaires needed for his evaluation process.

"We have been treating Jack with an ABA approach, so that if he does get a diagnosis of autism, our behavior treatment would not change much. Writing and reading are his biggest antecedents—his triggers—and by ignoring his meltdowns, we will extinguish the behavior," Caroline explained.

"As you have seen first-hand, Jack does not like this approach, and has escalated even further than when he was at school." Caroline referenced the knife incident. "What we would like you to do is to create a workspace for Jack. A separate room for him to work in."

"What is an ABA approach?" I asked.

"Applied Behavior Analysis. It is the process of applying behavioral interventions to shape maladaptive behavior in a systematic way, relying on data and proven scientific principles," Caroline said point blank.

I looked over at Mike.

"We don't have an extra room that we can designate for his own space. We don't have a finished basement or anything like that available," Mike said.

"Because we are going to be extinguishing these behaviors, seeing where they have gone and where he has been willing to take them, he needs a space where he can work, have a meltdown, deescalate, and recover. Having a room separate from his brothers that he can be contained in is key. During this extinction burst, Jack's behaviors will get worse before they get better."

Containment. Deescalate. Separate.

The conversations went back and forth, and it was decided that my older son's room would be the best option. The two oldest boys could share a room, just like the younger two kids. We would have to remove all of Kieran's belongings. The room would be sparse, consisting of a worktable, two chairs, books and a couple of games. Ainsley would bring a tote of teaching supplies with her when she came back once we have the room set up. Jill was ordering blocking pads to protect staff (and us) from any bouts of aggression. Since Jack had been restrained in his old school we had decided—unanimously—that we would not restrain him unless he was in danger or we were trying to get him into his study room. In taking this approach, Jack would have the freedom to be more physical and, in the past, he had hit and kicked his teachers, hence the need for the pads.

"I will take the data we have collected and craft a Behavior Intervention Plan that will outline the procedures to follow during Jack's non-compliant behavior. It is important the plan be followed by the tutors and both of you. We will introduce him to a green, yellow, red strategy where he can start to recognize when he feels deregulated or frustrated. A concrete color system will help him identify his feelings and access tools he can use for self-regulation." Caroline looked over at Jill.

"And I will go over this system in a social story with Jack and post visual cues for him around the image of a stop light," Jill added.

Caroline shifted topics and asked about how his brothers were doing in light of all that had happened at school and home. I shared that I was picking up Aidan at the end of the school day and that both of his older brothers still at the Bradford School had been put in situations where kids had questioned or made fun of their brother. No staff had met with or offered any support for either of the boys.

"It is important to have ongoing conversations with the other children affected within the family. It is confusing and hard to understand, and I would be happy to come and talk with them about it—if you want me to. Especially since we are gearing up for an extinction burst," Caroline offered.

Both Mike and I agreed that having her come by, without Jack there, to answer questions and talk with them was a great idea.

"It's been a few days since we have seen him. How has he been?" Jill asked, straightening herself in the chair as a brown spear of hair dangled near her eye, falling free from her short-cropped cut.

"He's been okay. I mean, a little edgy, but he has not had any huge outbursts or pulled a knife on anyone... Speaking of knives, should we remove the knives out of the kitchen?" As the words spilled out of my mouth, I heard how ridiculous they sounded. I couldn't help but feel like the naïve mother, the one in denial, that I used to judge.

"Yeah, that's a good idea. Actually, any sharp object should be removed. And any nick-knacks or breakable items should also be removed," Caroline gracefully responded to my seemingly stupid question.

As we drove away from the office, I had a strange sense of relief, and felt validated for the first time after all the times I had wondered and worried. I was also struck by the realization that we were just at the beginning and there was a long road ahead of us. I leaned my head against the car window and welcomed the blackness of the sky to consume me, closing my eyes as we drove home.

10

THE MISSING PIECE

Mike and I sat on the red leather couch in Dr. Anna Chambers' office. The air conditioner whispered through the vent in the wall next to me, but I still felt flushed. Dr. Chambers sat in a chair behind her desk with papers fanned across it, presumably ones with Jack's results. She was in her early forties, an attractive woman with light brown hair pulled loosely into a bun. She began the feedback meeting by noting strengths and differences that she had found during the recent neurological evaluation conducted over several sessions during the past few weeks. After she reviewed each test there were characteristics and behaviors he presented across the board —his inability to self-regulate, his inattentiveness and distractibility levels, his compulsive and sharp behaviors, and his rigidity and obtuse nature.

"Anna, is this a child that is on the autism spectrum?" Jane, our educational advocate, chimed in via speaker phone.

"Well, I am trying to get to that, Jane." Dr. Chambers

responded with an awkward smile. We laughed nervously, as we too were anxious to know more.

"As we pull all this information together – Jack's poor emotional regulation, low frustration threshold, organizational challenges, difficulty with fine motor tasks, his lack of understanding non-verbal cues, the large discrepancy between his language and math abilities, his previous diagnoses, and the fact that his I.Q. is in the superior range, I see a pattern has emerged," she paused and surveyed us with her brown eyes, taking our collective pulse. "After going through the tests, evaluations and observations, I feel his profile falls on the autism spectrum. Now, Jack is high functioning, probably more in line with Asperger's syndrome, but because of the potential changes in the DSM-V, his diagnosis is autism."

Her face was soft and filled with compassion. I imagine that this is not the first time she delivered this news to eager, tearful parents.

Someone had finally given my son the diagnosis I had been wondering about for years…her words continued to replay in my mind… "his diagnosis is autism."

"I know these may be hard words to digest. How are you doing?" Her kind eyes connected with mine.

"I feel like we finally have something that makes sense. It sounds strange, but I think the diagnosis is reassuring. I feel like he has brushed against it many times, but no one wanted to confirm it," I said.

"In regard to his recent diagnosis of anxiety and depression, these are a byproduct of Jack's autism—autism that had gone untreated—until now," she said as she shifted in her chair.

"Good. We have a diagnosis that we can take to the district, a diagnosis that will help guide the appropriate services and protect Jack. They have been perseverating on the fact that Jack has diagnoses of anxiety and depression, wanting to place him in a behavioral/emotional program, a placement that would be more harmful as these kids are far more debilitated and affected emotionally than Jack." Jane's tone teetered between irritation and elation.

As I listened to Jane, it triggered me back to our most recent team meeting. At the end of the meeting, Jane brought up that we, Jack's parents, had scheduled (and were paying for) a neuropsychological evaluation to be administered by Dr. Chambers.

"We may be dealing with a child on the autism spectrum, and if that is the case the lens of how the district is looking at Jack may need to be adjusted," Jane explained.

Mr. Rafferty looked thoroughly confused by this statement. His eyes quickly glanced around the table.

"Has anyone else on Jack's team seen any signs of autism?" His eyes searched each one of the professionals who sat around the conference table.

"I have," said Caroline Chase and gave a half-extended hand raise.

"Me, too," nodded Jennifer Booth, the school behaviorist.

Everyone else was silent. Took notes. Looked at their hands. Glanced at the two behaviorists who spoke up. This was a question that should have been asked months and months ago. No one else said a word.

I know why Jane felt enraged. When I looked around the conference room that day, I knew. The expressions on the faces of the professionals who didn't speak, spoke volumes. They knew that something wasn't typical with Jack. They knew they couldn't reach him. Maybe they didn't have the educational specialization to name it. Certainly, (aside from the behaviorists) it wasn't in their job description to diagnose him with autism; but, they knew. They all knew and said nothing.

I also knew why Jane was elated. Now we could finally help Jack. Laws existed that would help protect him because of his disability—a diagnosed, definable and concrete disability that a framework of supports could be built upon, and which the district would be held to in educating not only a child, but a child that required a specialized program that fit his learning style and needs. For Jane, it allowed her to do her job and get her client what was necessary for success. She was touched personally by autism. It ran deep. This was not just a job for her. This was her divine purpose.

"I know Caroline and her team of tutors and behavior specialists will help Jack through the next chapter. He has also been working with a specialized occupational therapist for writing and body regulation. She will continue to play a role in his educational programming."

"Will he need to attend a special school?" I asked.

"He may not be in a public school presently, but by having professionals who understand autism and consistently use a behavior plan tailored for him, he will begin to thrive. It will take time, but I see much potential in him—in his future. There is absolutely no reason why Jack cannot be educated in a public-school setting once his behaviors are curbed and the proper supports are in place."

Dr. Chambers sounded certain of this—of Jack, his diagnosis and his potential. Her words had power. They gave me hope.

Hope and validation. Questions that had pulled me, pushed me, for so many years, I now had answers for—validation that we were on the right path with Jack. Validation that we were good parents—mindful, loving and strong—who believed that there was a *reason* Jack ran from school that day. A *reason* for his "unpredictable" behavior.

We anticipated Jack would come out of the evaluation with some type of diagnosis. What I didn't anticipate was finding out how bright my son was. I mean, I always knew that he was smart, but I am his mother. Having the information measured and documented meant something. He was capable of learning how to adjust himself. He had the cognitive ability to understand and could be reasoned with. In the area of visual and spatial skills, his scores ranked in the superior category.

The testing not only gave me validation—something I needed to help me heal the past—it gave me courage. I could look at the results in black and white print and I could, for the first time in months, see Jack's future.

LATER IN THE WEEK, we found ourselves in a stretch of hot and humid weather, making us all a bit cranky. I decided to take the boys for a late afternoon swim ending with dinner beachside. The salty ocean water would be a remedy for the sticky weather. The boardwalk was a wooden bridge that extended over the marsh and creek to the beach. During high tide, the creek water was deep enough for jumping off the bridge of the boardwalk and for floating along the channel of the marsh. It was a place where these brothers found common ground. We had history here, years and years of making sandcastles and chasing seagulls. Of eating sandy peanut butter and jelly sandwiches and playing tag in and out the crevices of the marsh. It was our happy place.

I packed sandwiches and chips, and an apple or two, and we headed down. An evening high tide attracted fewer people, which made it less stimulating for Jack. Jack, at age seven, had been jumping off the bridge for two years. He begged me at four, but I held him off until five, only agreeing to his constant pleas if he wore a life vest. I remember treading water below the bridge as I watched his body vibrate with excitement as he stood on the edge that first time. He went quickly, his body thrust forward, plunging into the water before he bobbed up grinning from ear to ear. Gathering at the boardwalk, jumping, swimming and laughing brought us back. It helped us remember the best part of ourselves and how sweet life can be.

Patrick was already there. He had arrived earlier with a few of his friends. By now he was clearly out of food, probably money too, and came by to rummage through the cooler. At fifteen, he was slim and towered over me. He was a typical teenager, hanging out with friends and needing to be reined in from time to time. That spring he became a certified lifeguard and began working in a local town. Under his easy demeanor, I could see an alertness coming to the surface. He was becoming more aware, maturing into a man right before my eyes.

After he inhaled a sandwich, sucked down a juice box and chatted with me for a few minutes, he joined his brothers on the bridge. Jack noticed Patrick walking towards him on the bridge and waved at him to come closer.

"Patrick, watch this! Cannonball!" he yelled as he jettisoned his body off the side of the railing.

"Nice job, Jack!" Patrick replied giving him a thumbs up as Jack glanced up from the water below.

Even with cannonballs and summersaults galore, Kieran, hands down, had them all beat. He was our boardwalk daredevil. Kieran had an inner balance that he must have gotten from Mike. He scaled the railing and flipped off the top rail into the salty current below. He did other tricks too, which, as his mother, made my heart stop. But even with his risky maneuvers, Kieran was as cautious as a trained stunt man. I watched his eyes size up the area. His head nodded as he calculated his next trick. Over the past two summers, tourists, locals and kids have literally stopped dead in their tracks to watch Kieran jump off the bridge. I have heard folks mention him, not by name, but by his description and his crazy feats. It was amazing to see his level of control and focus.

Here, Kieran was confident. But he, too, struggled with writing and academics. He was also a sensitive kid and had his own way of figuring things out. I watched him as he teased Patrick, as younger brothers do. With a shove, off he went into the water. Patrick peered over the rail and Kieran tossed him a good-natured threat. Sometimes, they got on each other's nerves, but for the most part, they were friends, which was a good thing since they were sharing a bedroom due to Jack's need for a separate study area.

After Mike and I had met with Caroline and her team to discuss Jack, we came up with a plan to make the proposed changes palatable for the older boys. For Jack to have a study room, Kieran would need to move out of his room and into Patrick's. Jack and Aidan already shared a room, so, with four bedrooms, this would be the only option.

Mike called Patrick and Kieran into our room said, "how would you like to earn a hundred bucks?" he asked. "Each," he added.

"What do we have to do?" Patrick asked with his eyebrow slightly raised.

"It's easy. All you need to do is share your room with him," Mike said as he pointed to Kieran. "And all you need to do, is move in with Patrick," he said, looking at Kieran.

"For how long?" Kieran asked.

"Not long. Just for a few weeks..."

The older boys and Mike worked on breaking down bedframes and re-assembling the bunkbeds they thought they had grown out of, but it was the only option in Patrick's small room that would allow them both to have a bed and dresser. Everything else had to be removed from Kieran's room. We packed up belongings and moved them into the basement. We purchased a child lock for Kieran's closet, only to realize Jack had no problem cracking it open and dumping out whatever was left behind on the floor. The older boys weren't the only ones who had to adjust.

Aidan and Jack shared a room, giving Jack access to all of Aidan's things. I had Aidan put anything he valued into a cardboard box for safekeeping. The process of removing Kieran, prepping the room, and creating a safe work area for Jack took a couple of days to complete. The room was sparse in comparison to what it once was; only a table, wooden chair and, resting on the beanbag chair, a handful of books.

AFTER NUMEROUS DEATH-DEFYING jumps into the creek, the kids assembled on the blanket and wrapped themselves up in towels. The cooler was empty, daylight was fading, and the tide was going out. I leaned down and kissed the top of Aidan's wet head and felt his body shiver underneath my lips. We headed home for showers and to settle in for the night. It was almost bedtime for the younger two. Aidan beat Jack up the stairs and got the shower first. I can hear Jack's raised voice over the sound of the running water explaining why he should have gotten the shower first. I stood at the bottom of the stairs holding the cooler, not having made it yet to the kitchen to unpack and wondered if I would have to intervene. Would Jack accept coming in second? I heard the roll of the glass door and the spray of the water as the boys "switched" places. Although I dreaded seeing what condition the bathroom would be in with their tag-team antics, I was grateful there was no escalation.

Aidan came down a few minutes later and scooped himself a bowl of ice cream for dessert. I was at the counter cleaning out the cooler. All of a sudden, we heard a loud crash outside. It sounded like something smashed onto the metal basement bulkhead. I turned on the back lights and headed out to the yard. In the overgrown grass something glimmered.

"Mom, do you see that?" Aidan asked while trailing close behind me with spoon and dish in hand.

"What is it?" I said out loud as I walked over to the oblong-shaped object. Then, I knew.

"My lava lamp! How the heck did that get out here?" Aidan said in a frustrated tone, then his head tilted upward to the second floor.

"Oh, helloooo down there…It's me, J-A-C-K…Jack!"

In a flash Aidan ran into the house. I grabbed his arm and pulled him back, to try to reason with him. I could see where he was headed, and at that point, it could have escalated quickly. I corralled Aidan to sit on the couch and instructed him to take a minute to cool off.

"It's not fair! He broke my freaking lava lamp! The one I just got for my birthday from Grandma! WHY would he do that? Is he stupid or something? Why does he act the way he does?" Aidan burst into tears. His level of frustration was palpable. I felt his pain.

"I know you are frustrated and have every right to be. It's not okay for him to toss your things out the window. I am sorry it happened," I said.

"He's just a little jerk!" he said forcefully through his tears.

"I know it's hard to understand that Jack does things when he feels out of control. He takes thing too far and has difficulty regulating himself. But it does not mean he is stupid."

"Well, he does stupid things sometimes," said Aidan.

It was hard to argue with his logic, because tossing out a heavy glass object from a second story window wasn't a good choice. But it brought to my attention the need to revisit Jack's disability with Aidan to help him to understand. In hindsight the lamp should've gone into the box of breakables in the basement. I felt a tightness in my jaw, the pressure of the impossible task of anticipating Jack's every move. The weight of over-responsibility, of feeling guilty I wasn't able to predict his behavior, or the mistake of believing Jack would let it go and not retaliate towards his brother, was familiar. "I should've known," was a common response when Jack did something unexpected. I held myself accountable for Jack's actions and felt ashamed if I didn't intervene in time. And although I knew the importance of letting my other children know they were heard and supported during the throes of behavioral interventions, I found it challenging to do, because I was only partially present. I made promises I was unable to keep, which compounded feelings of failure. I was juggling a house, kids and Jack. Logistically there was no way in hell I could do it perfectly, but I was too exhausted and emotional to hear the call of self-forgiveness.

11

EXTINCTION BURST

a bead of sweat coursed down my scalp and onto the back of my neck. I stood in front of the closed door of Jack's study room. His tutor, Ainsley, was positioned directly across from me in front of the only window, which was also closed. Ainsley called me in when Jack refused to finish his work. Even though his session time only had another half hour, he couldn't hold it together. He paced around the room with clenched fists and his bare feet pounding into the worn blue carpet.

"I am NOT going to do my reading today! I don't NEED to! I already know how to read! You need to let me out of here!" His head tilted downward to trace his quick circular steps. I watched him with a keen eye waiting for his next move. Ainsley stood and looked toward the wall, keeping him in her peripheral vision, she stayed on point with the "ignore" directive of the Behavior Intervention Plan. I could see that she had placed his calming materials in the corner of the room next to his bean bag chair and a small pop-up tent.

"I am NOT taking a break either. I AM NOT IN THE YELLOW!" His voice screeched and his head bobbed upward. Catching my eye, he lunged full force at me. His arms were extended in front of him as he rammed his body into me. *Look away, look away! No eye-contact!* His small hands pushed against me as I directed my gaze to the far wall. I struggled to hold my body in place. The doorknob dug into my spine and kidneys while he moved me side to side. I positioned my feet further apart trying to gain balance. Jack noticed the change in my stance and responded; with closed fists, he began to punch me in the stomach, sides, and face. I stood my ground, my face stung, my sides sore from his small, yet powerful blows.

"Look at me, Mother! Can't you see what you're doing to your own son?"

Jack swiftly reached up and pulled my hair with both hands. I moved my head and leaned away, breaking his grasp. His fingers found my throat and squeezed. I looked down at him, over his tightened hands and stiff arms. His face taut, his actions desperate. Where was my baby boy?

DAYS BEFORE, Jack's behaviorist, who was in charge of his home programming, called to check in with me. We had implemented a new behavior plan and increased the demands on his academics. As I stood looking for my little boy, I realized Caroline's call was more of a warning shot.

Jack was being educated in our home, and under the guidance of Caroline, we implemented a revised version of his Behavior Intervention Plan (BIP). Once Caroline's team presented a structured academic curriculum and held Jack accountable in completing the assigned work, he began to exhibit increased behaviors. In the public-school setting, when Jack refused to finish his work, the teacher let things slide a bit. Once Jack got wind that this strategy worked, he branched out into other areas: refusing to take spelling tests, do his reading, or complete other routine tasks. If he refused, threw his paper or his pencil, he was rewarded by the teacher not holding him to the task. Once they recognized that this had become a pattern, they started insisting he comply. The classroom helper or school social worker hung over him and pointed out what he needed to do. Jack, who had a diagnosis of sensory processing disorder, later described what it was like to have an adult drape over him and how he felt their body press into him, and he couldn't breathe. Jack became more anxious due to the physical proximity of the social worker, which prompted Jack to escalate. He cleared desks, threw books, hid under tables and in his cubby. School staff were called to remove him from the classroom. During one episode, his special needs teacher had him in a one-to-one hold, to keep him under control. The administration had taken a reactive role with Jack—feeding into his behavior by calling me to the school to pick him up as he "earned" another suspension. In the end, academics were avoided, and he got a ticket home.

"It will take a lot of undoing. The school—time in and time out—reinforced Jack's maladaptive behavior. He will do whatever he can to get out of these non-preferred tasks. I have seen kids punch, kick, and bite and even defecate on the floor during an extinction burst," Caroline explained over the phone.

"We saw heightened reactions from Jack at school. I know that you have seen some of that at home too, but you need to prepare yourselves. It is going to get much worse before it will improve. But I promise you, if we stick to the intervention plan, it will get better." I knew that Caroline had been trying to prepare me, but her words fell short of the actual experience.

I FELT a sharp tug and then a release as my silver chain and mermaid charm broke free into Jack's hand. I stared beyond him, looking over to Ainsley, but still able to keep him in view. He saw the necklace snarled in his fingers. He paused; I sensed a hint of regret, only to be shattered by the sound of metal hitting the wall. He pivoted his body around to face Ainsley.

He launched himself forward, attempting to shove her away from the window. He grunted, yelled, and pushed—she moved ever so slightly; her body remained passive, it absorbed the shock and then returned to its form. She stood tall with her feet hip-width apart, her arms hanging in front of her with her right hand holding her left wrist. Jack stood in front of Ainsley and leaned his body into her left side. He positioned his feet, trying to press her away from the window. Abruptly, her eyes darted downward. She unclasped her hands and pushed her arm forward against Jack's face.

Did he bite her? Oh my God, he bit her!

As Ainsley regained her position and looked away from Jack, he took his fists and started to hit her repeatedly. I watched in horror, still stationed on the other side of the room, only a few feet away from my son who was beating his tutor. His hands struck her. His body slammed into her. His mouth, ripe with contempt, spewed nasty words. Meanwhile, Ainsley appeared unaffected by his attempts to derail her. She maintained her removed and detached composure, separating from him and his violent actions. Tears streaked down my face. I felt ashamed and helpless. The behavior plan made it clear that I was supposed to ignore what was happening, to allow him to strike her. But I was embarrassed and mortified that my child was acting out aggressively toward another person. These actions were never condoned in our home. Even with four sons, it was never okay to slap one another. This was different. Jack was different. I looked away for a minute and wiped the tears from my cheeks.

"I am going to jump out the window! Don't make me do this!" Ainsley drove her body back pushing Jack just out of reach of the swivel lock on top of the windowpane. Jack tripped over his feet and fell onto the floor. He looked up to see if there was a reaction. I continued to stare at the wall but watched him out of the corner of my eye.

"Don't you care, Mother? Don't you see that I just fell? That I could be hurt?"

I said nothing. He stood up and walked over to me. He paused for a few seconds and peered up into my face. A sudden sharp stinging sensation lanced my chin and cheek. And with that last strike, Jack collapsed like a skyscraper being demolished, folding into a heap of rubble onto the floor.

"You don't love me! How can you do this to me? I am your son..." He continued on with this line for several minutes. I felt torn. I was disheartened that we were here, that my son felt he needed to do this, and that he was acting out in ways that I am sure didn't make him feel good. I was also annoyed by his attempted manipulation. Words he spouted off, about loving him and seeing him in pain...of course it hurt me to see him that way! To see him distressed. My skin crawled in my own discomfort. I wished that I could click my heels together and return to Kansas. But I was not in Kansas anymore. I was here. There was no quick fix. The only way out was through.

I didn't respond to his baiting. His sullen tone began to elevate once more.

"I have to pee! Let me out of here." He got up and proceeded to reach around me groping for the doorknob. He stood up with his hands over his private area. I looked over at Ainsley, wondering what she was going to do. Would she allow him to go to the bathroom? Maybe he really did have to go. She continued to ignore him, he cried and pleaded to leave and use the toilet.

"Okay, you asked for it!"

And with that, he dropped his pants in the middle of the room and peed on the floor. I could hear the stream collect in a puddle on the carpet. As I processed the act that was occurring, I couldn't help but wonder if we had taken it too far. Then again, from my experience with preschoolers (as well as my own children), I had learned that the bodily functions, such as peeing and pooping, could manifest into behavior-driven reactions to the child's need for control during the potty-training phase. Could this be the case for Jack? Although he had been trained for years, was he purposefully peeing in an effort to control the situation? To avoid and escape?

Jack's outbursts reverted back to crying and bargaining. We remained stationed at our posts. Ainsley removed her cell phone from her shorts pocket, appearing to check the time. There was no clock on the walls. No reference point in Jack's study room. In fact, it was pretty sparse—table, chair, books, and materials. We had to strip down the room, even removing the ceiling fan after he hung from it during his first meltdown after we reconvened his sessions. Mike had to stop at Home Depot on his way home from work that first evening to pick up a replacement for the light and fan. After the kids were in bed, he removed the broken fixture and installed a single light fixture flush mounted to the ceiling.

Jack took his bean bag chair and shoved it into the play pop-up tent in the corner of the room. His hand reached out from the tent and grabbed a Koosh ball from a basket of sensory items. Maggie had suggested we compile a handful of objects that he could access when he was in yellow and use for calming his body and brain. Jack liked to hide when he was escalated. When he shut the world out, he lessened the visual input that he received. The beanbag provided pressure, the seat wrapped around his sides, and held him securely in place. The Koosh ball with its unique texture and bright color gave Jack an object to focus on —he was focusing his energy somewhere else, allowing time to deescalate—to regulate his body and mind.

"How much longer?" he asked. His tone was even and soft. Ainsley glanced down at her phone again.

"You're doing a great job, Jack. Five more minutes." Her voice was kind and pleasing.

Jack finished his break and climbed out of the purple play tent. Ainsley directed him to pick up the game materials he had tossed after rejecting his reading work. He was agreeable, chatted away, asking her what books they were going to read. I brought in the portable carpet cleaner to clean up the pee-soaked rug. Ainsley gestured to me and nodded her head toward Jack.

"Good job cleaning up all those pieces. Now you need to clean up the carpet." She pointed over his shoulder and he turned around to see the machine and the soiled rug. He made a face, a knee-jerk reaction to cleaning up his urine, but it quickly melted away. He asked if he could use the machine and I said okay. He gleefully used the wand—scrubbing, soaking, and sucking up the mess. Once the room was put back into order Ainsley directed him to the pile of books that had ignited his explosive behavior.

"Which one should we read first?" Jack said, joyful to go back to reading the books that had given him angst forty-five minutes before. Ainsley gave me a signal that I could leave—I walked out after I saw the two of them nestled into the corner on pillows reading. Jack leaned his head into Ainsley 's shoulder. Her arms encircled him, holding the book out so that they could both see the illustrations. She read a few lines, then it was his turn. It was part of their routine, a framework that consisted of academics with a couple of breaks scheduled in reinforced with *Jack's Choice,* opportunities he had to earn. The BIP, schedule, visual cues and reinforcements were all a part of Caroline's grand scheme to curb Jack's behavior. We were all to follow the same procedures of waiting him out, even when Jack was not in tutoring sessions, which was the remaining twenty-two hours of the day.

AINSLEY MET me at the door. She had a large three-ring binder under her arm, a tote bag, and her water bottle. Jack had tolerated the rest of the session with no incidents.

"I have Jack's binder and will log the data in from today's session. We ran late, so I will just take it with me and bring it back tomorrow. I would also like to review it with Caroline." She stood near the door, her stance relaxed, her demeanor laid back.

"I am so sorry about today." I apologized. My gut was twisted with guilt and shame. Even though intellectually, I knew these outbursts stemmed from autism, the mother in me still felt responsible. I was fearful she would leave us due to his behavior. Her stance was relaxed, and her eyes softened as she looked at me. She explained Jack's heightened behavior today was a result of the boundaries we set around his compliance to complete his work tasks. She reminded me of what Caroline had said about shaping behavior. At school, his teacher and staff had reacted to his refusals by allowing him to escape work demands. Essentially, they were reinforcing Jack's maladaptive behavior. For months, Jack's behavior was shaped in the wrong direction and our job was to bend it back.

"We are in the process of extinguishing his behaviors of escape and avoidance. By us following the behavior plan, ignoring unexpected behavior, or bad behavior and giving him tools to help gain self-regulation, his behavior will shift."

"Today was tough, but he did get back on track," she scanned my face, then continued. "It will get better, Mrs. Donovan. Trust me, I have seen worse," she said smiling.

"Are you okay? He didn't hurt you, did he?" I asked quickly in desperate bursts.

"No," she said, looking down at her arm, revealing a few

small indents of teeth, but no broken skin. "If he does bite you, push your forearm into him—like I did—it will break the bond releasing his mouth," she instructed. "Well, I have to go to my next appointment. I will see you and Jack tomorrow."

Good God. It was only Tuesday.

12

HAVE FAITH

"Happy birthday!" Faith announced as I opened the car door, her wide smile and exuberant attitude filled up the space between us. We had planned to go out for drinks and food. I didn't want to go. My energy was depleted, and I had to hit the reserve switch just to make it out the door. I was overwhelmed with every aspect of our situation but being at home with Jack had been increasingly isolating. I knew going out would be good for me.

I got into her car and we drove off. Mike had just gotten home and even though I knew Jack and the rest of the boys were in very capable hands, I worried about another flare up. Would Mike remember the protocol? Would he follow it? Would one of the older kids have to help drag Jack upstairs to deescalate?

"Are you okay?" Faith asked. A look of concern washed over her face.

I couldn't speak. It was the first time in weeks someone asked me how I was doing. She was really asking, not a casual "how are you?" in passing at the local Stop & Shop. She really wanted to know. I was paralyzed. To answer the question, I had to look inward, and acknowledge my brokenness.

"You're not okay," she said and pulled the car off to the side of the quiet street.

She rested her hand on my arm and looked at me with kindness. Jumbled words rolled out of my mouth. The reality of my beautiful boy and his erratic behavior produced a deep hopelessness that hung heavy inside my chest. I began to expel the day's events—another epic meltdown. One that left me bruised. How he tore off my necklace again, the second time after it was repaired. How he pushed his bedroom screen free and tossed the chain out before I could get to the window to lock and block it. His tutor and I tried frantically to move heavier items out the door to prevent him from throwing them. Once Ainsley and I were in our designated positions, blocking the door and the window, he rammed into me with his body. "You need to let me out, mother! I am NOT going to do my writing today!"

I explained to Faith that Jack had not had an escalation of this level in a couple of weeks, but something set him off. *Ignore, ignore, ignore*…was my mantra. His powerful fists pounded into my stomach, thighs, and side of my face. I moved slightly to avoid blows; tears welled in my eyes. "I am going to punch you in the vagina!" *Ignore, ignore, ignore…no eye contact. No attention. Just breathe.* Not getting any satisfaction from me, he charged at Ainsley, who was blocking the door. He wrapped his hands on her throat, "I am going to strangle you!" His hands could not reach the circumference of her adult-sized neck; rethinking his attack strategy, he started to kick her. My stomach churned as I watched him attack his teacher, and I could do nothing about it. I felt helpless and scared.

Faith looked right at me, taking in every word I confessed. There was no denying how bad it was. No back pedaling and making excuses about why I was distant or seemed tired. It was out there now, all of it, even the climactic performance when Jack stripped off his clothing in a last-ditch effort to escape his work. As the words spilled out, fear seeped in. Was I afraid that she would judge me and not want to have her kids play with mine? I was not embarrassed. It was worse; I was ashamed. Ashamed of my child's behavior, I still struggled with the notion that it was my fault, that his behavior was directly related to how I was raising him and not his autism. Certainly, I was aware that others might view it that way, but not Faith.

When my words dried up, she took my hands in hers. Her eyes were soft and compassionate. A warm tear trailed down my cheek.

"You are an amazing mother. You are doing the right thing for Jack and he is going to come through this and succeed. He is so lucky to have parents like you and Mike. I am here for you and your beautiful family. I love Jack and believe in him. Our family is your family—*always.*"

Her passionate words vibrated through me. She was truthful and generous. What she gave me was unconditional love and acceptance. I was overcome with emotion, my shoulders shuddered, and I began to sob. It felt as though her hands reached inside my chest and held my heart. During the past couple of months, in the trauma of this ongoing situation, I had forgotten about her, and the friendship I could rely on. I had gone into survival mode.

She hugged me and didn't let go, even when I tried to pull away, she squeezed me tighter. I had been holding it together, shutting down to get through the day, hour, minute. And the reality was—when did I have time to fall apart? Jack was with me twenty-four-seven. And when I did have time away, it was behind closed doors talking about him with Mike or Jane. Family checked in, but I got the feeling that they were done hearing all the gory details of his meltdowns, and the district's lack of guidance. They wanted to press fast-forward and get on with the next. But we were stuck, embedded in the trenches. In all honesty, even the thought of explaining, answering the questions that followed, and listening to suggestions was too much for me to entertain. I was physically and emotionally spent.

After a few appetizers and a couple of glasses of wine, Faith dropped me off at the house. It was late. The house was quiet. I sat down on the sofa in the family room and clicked on the television. The lights and sounds of the show playing were no match for the familiar loop of thoughts that returned. The events of Jack running from the school played over and over. It was a vicious cycle of fear, doubt and insecurity regarding what had happened, what could have happened, and what was going to happen. I replayed our role as his parents—did we do enough? Should we have pressed more? My thoughts led me back to the professionals, the educational specialists that he had listed on his IEP for the past four years. Why had this happened? What did they miss? Why wasn't a behaviorist called in earlier? So many questions that left me filled with anger and resentment.

After my big night out with Faith, Mike suggested that I

contact my former therapist and find additional time in the week to get away from the house, schedules, laundry, and the kids. I scoffed at his suggestion, tried to make excuses and told him that he shouldn't worry about me, that "I was fine." Several hours later, I still felt pissed off about his suggestion. And then it dawned on me…I was angry because I knew he was right. I did need a break. I just didn't want to be told that I needed to do another fucking thing right now.

It was true that to orchestrate time away was difficult due to schedules, but the deep truth was that I was filled with dread at the thought of leaving the house without me there to monitor Jack's behavior. After I had talked myself back into the idea of taking an hour or so for myself, I noticed that Patrick was off most Fridays. Reluctantly, I mentioned this to Mike and Patrick after dinner. Mike penned it in ink on the calendar: "Mom out." No going back now…

On Friday, I met up with my friend, Sara, for coffee just over the bridge—fifteen whole minutes away. Sara and I had been friends for almost twenty years. She was around the age of my mother and I usually found her calmness and positive nature soothing. We chatted over hot coffee and muffins, taking turns between sips and bites.

After several minutes, I noticed I was straining to concentrate on what she was saying. Her voice became drowned out by the background noises, other conversations, clanging dishes, and the high-pitched sound of the cash register keypad. A strange sensation came over me. Pins and needles vibrated through my hands. A few seconds later, I noticed that my chest felt light—I couldn't catch my breath—like birds were fluttering inside my rib cage. Was I having a heart attack? Maybe if I slowed my breathing and focused on something, it would go away. I looked past my friend to a small print hanging on the wall. I took slow deliberate breaths. For a few seconds, the sensation seemed to subside, but then returned with a vengeance.

"Are you okay?" she asked with a look of concern.

"I—I—I can't breathe..." I pushed out.

I sat in the front seat of her station wagon as she drove me to the local hospital.

"Just put your head between your knees...try to breathe slowly. I am going to keep talking in hopes that it will distract you. I think you are having a panic attack."

I nodded and leaned forward. She talked about all kinds of things—her kids mostly—and grandkids. During the drive over, my breathing began to regulate. Along with listening to Sara, I prayed to God, as I sometimes do, usually when I am alone in the car or find myself in deep shit and need divine intervention. This, of course, was the latter.

We arrived, checked in, and by the time I was called into see the admitting nurse, who diligently took my vitals, I began to feel foolish. I was feeling better, but knew that I should stay anyway, to clarify what had happened. Sara had stepped out to call Patrick. She also called Mike, who left work immediately and met me and Sara at the hospital. I was examined by a doctor and he followed a protocol that consisted of blood work, an EKG, and a chest x-ray.

"The good news is that all your test results have come back normal." My eyes strained to focus on this abnormally tall slender man with thinning hair and a wide smile. The medicine the nurse had given me earlier made my eyelids weighted and sleepy.

"I believe you have experienced a panic attack. I recommend that you see your primary doctor and go over some strategies for stress relief. In the meantime, I have a prescription for you for Ativan. If you experience these symptoms again, you can take one of these pills and it will calm you; but be aware, that you should not drive or operate while taking them." His left eyebrow arched as he looked down at me where I lay on the gurney. I almost laughed out loud. So, let me get this straight: if I have another panic attack, and I am not home, I can take a pill and wait for someone to come and pick my sleepy ass up from wherever I am? Maybe at one of Jack's therapy sessions? Or better yet, an IEP meeting? I took my script, thanked the doctor, and left.

I knew the medication was not a solution for me, but I did take his advice and followed up with my primary doctor. I was drowning and I knew it. We discussed talk therapy. I needed a shift of perspective—a life raft—something.

I started to see Janet, a therapist. Her office was right down the street, making it convenient for me to catch a later appointment. It was there I would cry. I let down my guard and showed my vulnerability. I had desperately needed a place to vent and locate my feelings. It provided space for them to come to the surface, someone to help sort through the scattered pieces of myself.

After going over Jack's last day in school for the third or fourth time, she looked at me thoughtfully.

"I have been listening to you talk about Jack's escape from the school, how it was handled, and I keep racking my brain trying to figure out how these professionals had let it go this far. The only thing I can come up with is that, because you and your family have been a part of the school community for so many years, they were trying to work it out." She sat across from me in a seventies-style orange cushioned chair.

"Maybe they had the best intentions, but my son ran into the arms of a stranger! He ran away from the school! They did not keep him safe! They failed Jack! They failed us!" Tears streamed down my face; I reached for the tissue box and blow my nose.

"They should have done more for Jack," Janet said kindly. "They should never, ever, have let it go as far as it did."

There was a long pause. I sat quietly, absorbed her words of validation, honoring the stillness we found ourselves in, and soon realized how utterly exhausted I was. I leaned into it and became stagnant, like the creek at slack tide. I was motionless. I looked out the window of her office. The wind whipped through the tall, feather-tipped salt grasses, making them dance. I heard the faint rustling sound as they swayed to the silent music of twilight. The sea air crept beneath the cracked-open glass pane. Low tide was pungent but grounding me into the present moment.

Janet cleared her throat and brought me back.

"Where were you just now?" she asked.

"I used to take long walks in the woods, write poetry and journal. I knew who I was and how I felt. That person has slipped away. She seems so far away from me. It is only here where I can...find her." A tear streaked down my cheek.

She nodded thoughtfully.

"Have you ever thought about running?" she asked.

"Do you mean, like the sport?" I let out a small laugh.

"Yes, running. It can be a great way to lessen anxiety naturally, as well as giving you time to process and be outside, a place that seems to fill your soul."

"Hmmm... let me think about that."

We wrapped up the evening with a few other suggestions, including yoga and daily journaling.

"Return to your roots," she suggested. "That is your ticket home."

13

ZONES OF REGULATION

*H*e thrashed his body as we carried him up the staircase. Even with two sets of hands, it was challenging to get Jack into his study room. Patrick positioned himself at the door and I moved to the window. After Jack's screaming and cussing had subsided, he turned his anger towards me. I stood holding my space, detached from the pressure of Jack's hands and body, while he attempted to push me again and again. I glanced over to Patrick, who was following the procedure and ignoring his younger brother's pleas for attention. Patrick's eyes were looking in the direction of Jack, but not at him, keeping him in his line of sight.

As the eldest son, he was the peacekeeper and boundary setter for his siblings, a role often taken by the oldest in a big family, especially one with all boys. But this was not part of his job. At least, it was not what I envisioned as being a part of his duties as a big brother. *Did he just flinch?* Even though Jack was not hitting Patrick, he felt the hit. Underneath the façade of strength, Patrick too, was holding it together. A deep sadness stirred within me. Patrick had a front row seat, and I was sad—no, ashamed—to have to need him. To have him bear witness to the rollercoaster ride of Jack's extinction burst.

Before we implemented the new behavior plan, Caroline advised us to pack up any breakables, sharp objects, and valuables. She explained that once the plan went into place and we were actively reinforcing our expectations for Jack there would be push back. He would most likely go through an extinction burst, a term as used by behaviorists and behavioral psychologists, to describe a blast of defiance that occurs during the elimination process. Jack's behavior plan targeted two areas of maladaptive behavior: attention seeking and escape/avoidance. For Jack, by our blocking the egresses, we were denying him access to his maladaptive behavior of escape and avoidance. As we ignored his bids for attention through aggression and manipulation, we were not giving him power, and by not feeding the flame, we were extinguishing it.

I peered down at Jack who had stopped pushing me, and instead had planted himself on my feet, using them and my shins like a chair. I could tell by the slope of his shoulders he had become relaxed. I glanced at the time. Five more minutes. As if on cue, Jack rolled off my feet and found a book and began to leaf through it. Reading has a calming effect on him. When he was in the green zone, he could return to cleaning up his toys. It was imperative Jack return to the task he was doing prior to acting out as having him do so reinforced work expectations and the rules he needed to follow. By holding him accountable, we were shaping his behavior.

We had begun to see hopeful glimpses of Jack's behavior lessening—longer stretches between outburst (days, not hours), and shorter duration of the escalations themselves, which was reassuring. Atlas would be consulting with Jack's OT soon to create a sensory diet, which is a collection of materials and strategies he can access when he becomes dysregulated. The hope was that eventually Jack would learn to understand and identify earlier signs of frustration and anxiety before becoming explosive and out of control.

After five minutes with Jack remaining calm, I directed him to do a couple of compliance tasks within the study room to assess if he was back in the "green zone" and ready to return to the non-preferred activity that set him off. Patrick watched his brother stack the books neatly and roll his yoga ball into the corner. I gave a nod to Patrick, letting him know that we were good to go, and he opened the study room door. I told Jack to clean up his toys in the living room so he could earn a "Jack's choice" activity (a part of his schedule). He moved quickly around us and down the steps. I heard the sound of the building blocks being tossed into the bin. Yes, success!

"Are you okay?" I asked, turning my attention back to Patrick.

"I guess. I just don't understand why you let him treat you that way," he said with fleeting eyes.

"I know it's confusing," I said.

"But you don't even *say anything* to him. You just take it," Patrick said.

"True. But, when he is in a heightened state, he cannot hear me. And honestly, he knows. He knows he is not supposed to hit or hurt others. If I engaged, it would only lengthen his outburst," I said.

I could see he was mulling the information over.

"It is part of the way Jack is neurologically wired. He gets stuck in a loop. His rigid thinking produces anxiety and shows outwardly as defiance. Not to mention, Jack is reactive due to the trauma and conditioning he received at school prior to his autism diagnosis." I said, regurgitating the information I was given to help me understand my youngest, hoping it would begin to make sense for my oldest.

"So, he's not doing it on purpose?" he asked.

I could tell he was having a hard time buying what I was selling.

"No, in a matter of speaking. This is why we have professionals teaching us how to treat his behavior, because it is tricky and needs to be handled in a systematic way. Eventually, he will get to a point where he can recognize when he starts to get elevated—*before* he loses control." I said, as I searched his face for understanding.

Patrick's phone buzzed indicating a text message. He quickly read it and asked if he could meet the guys at the basketball courts for a pick-up game. As he was leaving, I thanked him, and mentioned I would be available to talk later if he wanted to. I knew he needed time to process Jack's diagnosis and what it would mean being his brother. Patrick was a fifteen-year-old sorting out who he was and who he wanted to be. He was beginning to define himself as a person and I wondered how this experience would change him. Or how it would change us all...

I thought about Aidan and our conversation after the lava lamp incident. How understanding Jack's autism, an almost invisible disability, was hard. It's not like he had blue hair and we could point and say that all kids with blue hair were on the spectrum. In recent years, the autism definition had become broader, encompassing many developmental delays underneath the autism umbrella, including Asperger's syndrome, which best described Jack. His autism was his own unique version. There were common traits among people on the spectrum, but they all had their own flavor. And for my own children, who have known Jack all of his life, they didn't see his differences so much, only his heightened behavior.

It was another topic area I could bring to Aidan's therapist, John. Aidan had begun seeing a mental health counselor, as Mike and I thought it would help him to have someone he could talk to. The decision came after to a call from Aidan's teacher who had become concerned after she recently noticed a decline in his social interactions. He was keeping to himself, especially on the playground, during recess. Other kids would be playing games and interacting, but not Aidan. He was often seen on the edges, either walking the perimeter of the grounds or climbing one of the structures away from peers.

Aidan was a happy, driven and sometimes impulsive kid. He was self-propelled and independent. He got excited about learning, and often pushed himself to achieve, in and outside of school. As a Cub Scout, Aidan set the bar high for his individual popcorn sales during the yearly fundraiser the previous fall. Jack was also in scouts and sold popcorn, but had difficulty going door to door and speaking with people. I marveled at how determined Aidan was to reach his sales goal. He was given top recognition and even awarded a prize for his efforts. Although Aidan was born with an inner fire, we also recognized the pressure he placed upon himself to reach his high standards.

Was the distance between Aidan and his peers a by-product

of his brother's removal from school? Watching his brother act inappropriately made Aidan feel he needed to stand on the sidelines in order to be seen as the good kid or not be seen at all, though of which I was not sure. Too many psychology courses in college made me overthink things. I tried to classify everything so it made sense, so I could apply a remedy or at least an understanding of the dynamics swirling around me. As a result, my maternal instincts had clicked into fifth gear. For years, I was the mom in charge of it all—from skinned knees, to jockeying school activities and sports schedules.

But now there was no amount of Neosporin I could apply to the wounds to take away the pain, to lessen the scarring, as this time it hovered just under the surface. There was no quick fix either. It would just take time. And lots of therapy.

I pulled into a space in the parking lot of the pond where Aidan was taking sailing lessons. Jack jumped out the slider of the van and ran to the playground that was located between me and the lake to wait for his brother. Windows down, I heard Jack's voice echoing as he climbed the structure and flew down the blue plastic slide. It was a hot sunny day and the rest of the kids were in the water. Maybe next time I'd remember our bathing suits so we could cool off. As I gazed out at Jack, I wondered if he was hot wearing his Angry Birds plush hat. He liked to pretend he was the black bomb bird, so he wore the ski hat, the one with the ear flaps and balls for tassels, when he was playing the part. Usually he played the game in our yard, building structures from the wood pile to create "houses" to be knocked down. He even had a green piggy stuffed toy he put into his act, but he'd left the pig home.

My cell phone rang. It was Jane. I knew she was calling to

touch base with me about Jack. I told her we had scheduled the consult between Caroline's team and his OT and asked her if there was anything I should bring up during the meeting.

"Make sure that Robin is looped in on any new treatment protocols they will be implementing. Robin has the behavior intervention plan but having the additional supports to use with Jack in her office will give Jack a high level of consistency," Jane said. "I want his home providers and therapist to be on the same page when we go into the school team meeting in August. How's Jack doing?"

"Jack is doing better. He is having fewer explosive behaviors and has acclimated to the summer schedule. He has a hard time with surprises and likes to stay on our schedule, but he has increased his level of tolerance for his daily tasks. Don't get me wrong, there is still push back, but it's not always a red behavior," I said.

"And his tutors are logging the data on this? On his behavioral programming?" Jane asked.

"Yes, I believe so. But I have not talked with either of the behaviorists since before the extinction burst," I said.

Jane continued on discussing next steps, one of which was touching base with Caroline and how we needed to address any potential pitfalls before the team meeting. Mike and I paid for Dr. Chambers to drive down from Boston to read the results of Jack's June neuropsychological report. Needless to say, there would be a lot of ground to cover with the report, Jack's autism diagnosis, and her recommendations for Jack's future placement. Jane wanted to make the most of our time by not getting sidetracked, or worse, surprised by any new unseen information. I was responsible for collecting and distributing any formal evaluations to be reviewed prior to every team meeting. Aside from being his mom, I was Jack's case manager, having ongoing conversations with Jack's tutors, behaviorist, counselor, occupational therapist and any other professional who was involved with Jack. It was my job to not only collect evaluations and make sure everyone was "on the same page," but I was also taking the informal reports, the ones given after a therapeutic session. Taking notes on scraps of paper in my car or on the back of bills I needed to pay during a phone call was commonplace. Synthesizing the information to find a formula for Jack was the goal and to have clear communication and a plan as we headed into the team meeting was how Jane would help get us there.

14

SENSORY DIET

aggie was at our home for an OT consult with Jack's tutors. She explained the goal of the consultation was to create a sensory diet—a collection of therapeutic activities Jack could access for self-regulation. Since Jack was now on the other side of the extinction burst, professionals could itemize what worked therapeutically and what did not, sharing information to create a comprehensive sensory diet. They gathered upstairs in Jack's study room. The three women, Jill, Ainsley, and Maggie discussed Jack's schedule, his motor breaks and additional tools that could be utilized in the home setting.

I stood in the hallway and took in the information. I felt as though I was a voyeur of sorts, curiously looking in from the outside. Materials mentioned were a body sock, pop-up play tent, wiggle spot, yoga ball, Thera-band and bean bag chair.

"Do you know what a body sock is?" Maggie asked. I shook my head.

"*This* is a body sock," she said as she held up a yellow tube of fabric. "It's a large, stretchy, pillowcase that he can pull on his whole body. He can push his limbs against the fabric and get sensory feedback."

She handed me the sock made from a silky Lycra material. Jack craved input. From the time he was a small child crashing into couch cushions was a favorite activity. Because Jack had Sensory Processing Disorder, his nervous system lacked the ability to synthesize the sensory input of his environment. He adapted his body by moving hard and fast through time and space. His feet pounded, he touched things roughly (and impulsively), and he was often found under his weighted blanket. When Jack accessed grounding tools like the sock or his weighted blanket, I noticed it calmed him.

"It seems like this body sock will not only provide the pressure he craves, but it looks like it will slow him down," I said while tugging on the fabric feeling its elasticity.

"Exactly! He will have to slow down and organize his thoughts and movements while getting into the sock, and while he is inside it, the act of pushing against it slows movement organically." Maggie's eyes sparkled as she talked.

"And the Thera-band?" I asked, eying a long strip of rubber.

"The band is the same idea. It provides resistance and feedback. I recommend tying this around the four legs of Jack's work chair. We have been using the band in my center when he is doing table work. It gives his feet and legs something to stretch while sitting in the chair. It has helped Jack focus longer."

"That would be great!" Jill chimed in. "Our goal is to get him table ready for a classroom environment. His body is kinetic and wiggly when sitting at the worktable. Writing is one of his antecedents—sets him off with behaviors as soon as you put a pencil in his hand. This may help build his tolerance."

"The wiggle spot is also a way to give kids input while sitting on a chair."

Maggie held out an inflated round disk that appeared to be made of exercise ball material. There were nubs on one side while the other side was smooth.

"Again, the idea is that the bumpy side provides sensory input. The reverse side is for kiddos that like to move while they are working. They can wiggle on the disc without getting up from their seat. For some kids being able to move expands concentration."

She handed me the round disc. I stood behind them in the doorframe juggling the body sock, band, and wiggle spot in my arms. They discussed the idea of creating a "quiet corner" with a bean bag chair and a handful of books. It made sense that he could access these materials during one of his therapeutic breaks. I understood how this could be implemented into his two-and-a-half-hour ABA tutoring session and wondered how it would it transfer to other times when his ABA tutors went home. How would it work on the days when he was arguing with me about getting into the car, or about going outside to play, or last week when he bolted from our parked car? I had to pull over because he had begun to kick the back of my seat. The van doors were locked, but as soon as I mentioned he needed to "take a break," he hit the button and opened the slider door. He ran lightning fast across the parking lot and onto the grass between the next set of buildings. I finally caught up with him and had no choice but to take him down on the front lawn of the Burbridge Water Department. Cars slowed down as I proceeded to drag my flailing seven-year-old's body back to the van.

Beads of perspiration swelled at my hairline as my clammy hands gripped the rubber band and plastic disc. I was out of my league. Parenting a typical child was challenging enough. How in the hell was I going to raise this child on the autism spectrum? What if I couldn't? What if it got worse? What if he stayed home forever and never went back to school?

Pins and needles traveled in waves from my fingers and toes toward the center of my body. Oh, God, do not let me have a panic attack now! Not in front of Jack's professionals. No. No. No… Just breathe…In and out. In and out. Their voices faded into the background. I slowly moved my body away from the doorframe into the hallway facing the bathroom. A whirlwind of negative thoughts twisted inside my head. I imagined Jack running away, out into traffic, getting hit by an oncoming car. I saw him lash out at me and punch me as he had done before. I saw him slumped over on the floor wailing and rocking back and forth…my heart pounded. I shut the bathroom door behind me and staggered to the side of the tub. The materials in my hands fell to the floor. With my knees spread, I leaned in between them and closed my eyes.

How would I remember to do all of what was required for his success? How was I going to execute the sequenced steps of his plan? How could I be the mother Jack needed? The mother he deserved? My chest was light, as if it were being lifted by winged butterflies. I concentrated on my breath, attempting to bring my anxiety down.

Several minutes passed. Once my breathing was even, I stood up and wiped a cold cloth on my face. My body was more grounded. I could no longer feel my heartbeat, no more pounding or fluttering wings, and the tingling sensation had finally subsided. This episode was much shorter than the previous one.

The therapists backed out of Jack and Aidan's room, the last room upstairs to be addressed during the meeting. Maggie looked at my face and returned a sympathetic smile.

"I know this is like a foreign language. Don't worry. I will type it out so we can use it as a reference." She reached out and touched my arm.

It was agreed that having the Zones of Regulation visuals posted at home and in his therapeutic settings would aid in providing consistent care. Jill handed out laminated copies to Maggie and me. She gave me an extra copy to deliver to Robin during our next session. Learning each color and its definition was the first step. Being able to identify when those feelings began to bubble was the second step. The descriptions identifying the maladaptive behaviors were taken directly from Jack's intervention plan. If he was in "yellow," we all would have a clear understanding what it looked like and how to respond. Caroline's intention by scaffolding his care was to provide a seamless treatment for Jack across the board.

"These visuals will not only help us; they can be used as a guide for you and your family. I know that he has had meltdowns when we are not here and you have had to treat them at home, or even on-the-go," Jill said, as she looked at me.

"Yes, on some days when he had a relatively smooth session with Ainsley, he would have a behavior afterward or even before the session. Getting him into or out of the car has proven to be challenging. Yesterday he refused to get into the car and climbed up the hood and sat of the roof."

"What did you do?" asked Maggie.

"He was on the roof of the car in the garage," I started. "I feared when he did come down there were tools and things that he could throw. I had no choice but to wait him out. I ignored him and he came down about thirty minutes later. I blocked the door and reminded him that we had to go to the playground then back afterward for tutoring. I reminded him that to get to his afternoon screen time we had to do these things first. He then got into the car and we went." I shrugged.

"The heightened level of behavior has decreased, but as Nicole mentions, we will still see behaviors. He will continue to try to avoid academics or non-preferred activities. As we adopt this system of regulation, implement the sensory diet and follow the procedures outlined in his behavior plan, they will continue to decline."

"So, red behavior is aggression, destruction, and elopement?" Maggie asked.

"Yes. Remember that he never starts with that, you can see and hear it building up. Now, the trick is getting him to buy into taking the yellow breaks," Jill replied.

Nope, never started at red. I thought back to the team meeting after his escape from school, when a school staff member said, "his behavior came out of nowhere!" No, it didn't. How had they missed the signs? I felt my own elevation return. I took a couple of long breaths to slow myself.

"I have some great motor activities that provide the deep pressure he loves. I'll print out a copy and give it to Nicole tomorrow when Jack has OT. Does that work for you, Nicole?"

I heard Jack's voice travel up the staircase. He was scripting a Sponge Bob episode in pounded breaths, like he was working out. He must have been bouncing on the yoga ball again...

"Nicole?"

"Oh, sorry. Yeah, we will be there tomorrow."

JILL AND I stood in the driveway after we say goodbye to Ainsley and Maggie. Jill wore multiple hats at Atlas Educational Services. She was not only a teacher and ABA therapist, she was also part owner.

"You look a little peaked. Are you okay?" she asked, looking over at me.

"I just feel on edge all the time. I'm never sure if Jack is going to have a behavior. It is especially challenging when we are out in public or driving the car. I am scared that I won't be able to handle him or that he'll create a scene and opportunities for other parents and kids to judge him. Or worst-case scenario— he'll get hurt."

Her eyes were kind and full of compassion. She stood there and listened to my concerns.

I continued. "I'm afraid I won't implement the plan properly. That I'll make it worse and his behavior will drag on and on..." My words rushed out of my mouth at a quick clip; upon hearing my own desperation, I was embarrassed at how unhinged I sounded.

"We do the best we can in the moment. We have a protocol, and we follow it to the best of our ability. You are doing great. Jack's extinction burst was a long one, but he is getting the hang of it, because we have reinforced that no matter what behavior he pulls, he will, without a doubt, return to the work or activity that he is avoiding. You are with him the majority of the day and his behavior modification comes from the things that you are doing with him at home," Jill explained.

Although her words were reassuring, my uneasiness lingered.

15

UTOPIA

*I*t was the beginning of August. Our team collected at the school to discuss Jack's home programming and to listen to Dr. Chambers read Jack's neuropsychological results from his June testing. We paid for this evaluation ourselves, which allowed for ample time to formulate a strategy for the meeting. I was learning that there was a bit of "sport" involved, planning was strategic, like a good game of chess with a seasoned opponent. We wanted to be several moves out before our feet crossed over the school entrance threshold.

Our educational advocate recommended we invite Dr. Chambers to read her report. Jane was concerned that having the school staff psychologist read the report could lead to misinterpretations, and if any questions arose, she couldn't answer them in certainty. It was hard to deny that the added expense was not ideal in our current situation, but Mike and I agreed that we did not want any leeway in the interpretation of the document.

A small group assembled in the library. It was summertime,

which meant that only the key players from the school district would attend the meeting. The home support team was present to update everyone on Jack's progress.

Caroline indicated Jack was through the extinction burst. In a happy but cautious tone, she reported no maladaptive behavior over the last several days and added that they had been able to increase the length of his sessions to three hours. Robin shared she had seen his generalized anxiety decrease and they were working on naming specific areas of anxiety. Once they were identified she would provide specific strategies for working through them.

Dr. Chambers read through Jack's neuropsychological evaluation and pointed out that Jack struggled in the area of social cognition: social boundaries, age-appropriate conversations, scripting, theory of mind (difficulty taking another person's perspective), and self-regulation. She didn't feel that the behavioral component was typical of him but felt that he developed anxiety due to his lack of social knowledge. She looked up from her notes and paused.

"Jack is a child with high-functioning autism. His anxiety and behavior stem from his autism and, because of this, he is not able to access his education."

She suggested a slow transition into a small setting with professional staff knowledgeable in high-functioning children on the autism spectrum. She recommended a language-based classroom he could transition into for social opportunities with a familiar staff member, like one of the Atlas staff trained in his behavior plan. In addition, he needed a full behavior plan reflective of his school environment and a designated area for de-escalation. A "fresh start" with peers who didn't know his behavioral history would be key. Lastly, hard data, not observations, which are subjective, should be the driving force for the transition back to the classroom.

Upon hearing Jack's diagnosis and recommendations, Mr. Rafferty responded by saying the district doesn't have the "utopian" classroom setting mentioned in the report. He requested that the school behaviorist work collaboratively with Caroline to help determine transition. This would consist of weekly home visits by district staff to observe Jack.

The meeting did not end there. It went on and on. Suggestions about possible educational placement were tossed around. Ideas ranging from out-of-district placement (another collaborative school with a therapeutic environment), to a different public school in town. Jane, Caroline, Robin, and Dr. Chambers all supported the idea of Jack being integrated back into the public-school system; they echoed the belief that, with the proper supports, Jack would acclimate and be successful. Caroline admitted there was work to be done to get Jack ready for a typical learning environment. Jill reported he was able to sit for ten minutes at the table for a preferred task and five for a non-preferred task. He could read (taking turns) for up to thirty minutes sitting in a bean bag chair with his weighted blanket. After a few more rounds of brainstorming placement ideas, the meeting adjourned until the first week in October. It was clear Jack would not be starting back to school in September and, coming out of the roller coaster discussion we just had, no one was certain of when or what his future placement would look like.

Even the professionals who agreed that he could be placed in a public-school setting with proper supports were at odds with where to start. One person mentioned a social skills group to be held at one of the three elementary schools in town. Another professional thought that Jack was not ready for social feedback from peers. It was finally decided that Maggie would pair him up with another student at her clinic. She would have the two work together during their scheduled OT sessions each week. This was our steppingstone. Even though Jack had been making progress at home with tutoring instruction, this would be the first opportunity for him to work with another peer.

Even though Jack was making progress, we had a long road ahead of us. Sitting in the room and witnessing the indecisiveness of the professionals that were forging Jack's educational programming left me nervous and disappointed. Not only was the path unclear, the steps to get anywhere were incrementally very small. In one respect, it was good that they were small, allowing time for him to continue attaining skills and knowledge about himself. It was frustrating because I felt like he was losing time. Each day he was not in a school environment, it was detrimental to his social and academic growth. One peer was great to begin with, but if the peer was getting OT services, he was not a neuro-typical child either. Jack needed peer models he could learn from.

16

LEFT BEHIND

*T*raced up the stairs to take a quick shower before Jack's scheduled tutoring session with Ainsley. We were running behind after our delayed trip to the library. Jack refused to get out of the van to pick out his weekly supply of books. Instead, he placed the canvas book tote over his head.

"I am not going in there one more time!" Jack yelled firmly with his arms across his chest in protest.

"Jack, you are in *yellow* and now need to take a break."

He kicked the back of the seat and started humming loudly.

After a few minutes, the humming transitioned into a quieter hum, making way for his imagination to take hold, he began to script what appeared to be a scene from a movie he had watched the night before. Apparently, he was diving down deep to find the city of Atlantis, or at least that was what I could glean from his chatter. After ten minutes or so, his voice subsided, and he removed the tote from his head. His body was calm and relaxed. His face had softened. He was back into *green*. After only ten

132

minutes, he was back in *green*. Ironically, the tote he placed on his head had the same effect as the tent had in his sensory corner in his room. It blocked out harsh light and sound, giving him a chance to reorganize and regulate his body.

"I am ready to go inside, Mother. Let's get this over with, oh and by the way, you can pick out the books," he stated a matter-of-factly.

He always said this—that *I* could pick out *his* books. It was his way of controlling an uncontrollable situation. His way of setting boundaries. Today, it was his way of protesting that he was not at school with his friends. That was what he missed most —the kids. We were at the beginning of a new school year and Jack was left behind.

A week before the start of classes, Jack and I were waiting for Ainsley on the front steps.

"Well, I won't be seeing Ainsley much longer now," Jack announced in a casual tone. We had been instructed to wait to tell him until a couple of days before school began. His behaviorist had advised us not to break the news to him until right before school opened. In the past, the more time he had to ruminate over upsetting news, the bigger his reactions had been. But, with him assuming he would be attending school soon, I feared he would react stronger if we lied about it.

"Jack, you know that Dad and I are looking for the best possible school for you, right? We have seen a few different places and are working with Miss Caroline and your team to find one that is right for you." He sat with his hands twisting in his lap, his gaze distant.

He began to cry, his words muddled in between sobs. I could only decipher fragmented thoughts of missing his friends and how lonely it would be at home without his brothers. My heart tumbled out of my chest and cascaded down our brick steps. Unfortunately, there was nothing I could do but to hold him. There was nothing I could do but to keep showing up and pushing our agenda forward for an appropriate educational setting. There was nothing to do but to keep him grounded in reality, saying the hard things even when his feelings could get big—even explosive.

There were times during this process of reshaping him, times like on the front steps, when I could feel the weight of his sadness, I wanted to absorb it into my body and ease his pain. But the truth was, I needed to allow him the dignity of his own feelings. Denying or sugar-coating wouldn't be in anyone's best interest, and if he was driven to be at school with peers, maybe it would reinforce his willingness to buy into the raised expectations.

ONCE WE GOT inside the library, he played with the toys for a few minutes, and when I reminded him to pick out three books, he scurried off in search of his favorite Dav Pilkey series, *Captain Underpants*. Three books would not be enough. I picked out the majority of the books for our weekly read. At first, I chose randomly, but after a few weeks, I realized I needed a better plan, as I couldn't remember which books I had taken out the weeks prior. Had we read *Zen Shorts*, yet? Or was that a different one with a panda on the cover? I stood in section "K," and began to choose thirty to forty books, filling up our large tote. Jack had a keen visual memory and it was discovered that he remembered the pictures and upon reading or, hearing a book read, he could repeat the text from memory on the second time through without reading a single word.

We met at the counter and Jack saw Mr. Peters. Mr. Peters was somewhat famous—he had won a national award for being the top children's librarian in the country. Everyone loved him, especially Jack.

"Hey, Mr. Peters. Remember me, Jack Donovan? I was in your story hour, you know, when I was little?" Jack's palms turned upward, questioning.

It was curious to me, that each time Jack saw the librarian, he would address him this way—as if to jog his memory. Jack liked to help hold the books so he could use the wand to read the bar codes.

"Okay, Jack, last one—you get to zap it!" Mr. Peters handed over the scanner gun and Jack pressed the button and laughed. My heart warmed as I watched their joyful exchange.

"You know, you're the only one who lets him do that here, that is why you are his favorite," I joked.

"How do you think I get them all to come back? Job security," he winked.

___

JACK ASKED to swing on the swing set before tutoring began and, with no protests about being outside or about tutoring, I viewed it as a win. I took a lightning-fast shower, finished getting dressed, and pulled my hair back into a towel. I stood at my bedroom window, watching him swing and sing to himself through the screen. I decided to towel dry my hair and go with a ponytail. A minute or two later, I grabbed a water bottle and headed outside. To my surprise, he was not on the swing in our side yard. I scanned the perimeter, and after a few seconds, I heard his voice and a shearing spray of water. My eyes turned in the direction of the enormous RV parked in front of my neighbor's house. The sound of the hose hitting the steel construction of the RV echoed across the cul-de-sac. I walked over, figuring maybe Jack was on the other side with Jim...then I looked up.

Oh, my God! The roof! Jack and my neighbor were on the roof of the RV! By the rate and speed of the debris jettisoning off the edges of the camper, Jack must have had the garden hose setting on *power wash*. Did Jim understand how unpredictable Jack could be? Did he have any idea Jack struggled with motor planning and had an undeveloped sense of where he is in space? Did he realize that he, himself, was in danger of Jack accidentally knocking him off to fall to his death?

"Now, Jack...don't go too far over now...come this way," Jim pointed, gesturing where to stand.

"Okay, Jim, I'm coming right to you!" Jack exclaimed while grinning from ear to ear. More water and tree droppings splashed off of the RV.

Jim continued to direct him, speaking calmly but loud enough to be heard. Jack was focused and listening to Jim's requests. I stood on the street and looked up at them. I found myself horrified and equally amused by this scene playing out above me. Jim had been our neighbor for years. He had kids and grandchildren. All of them knew Jack because Jack had never been shy. When Jim was out tinkering with some project, Jack ran over to check it out. If the grandkids were over and they were swinging on Jim's rope swing (or even if they weren't) Jack invited himself over for a swing…or two…or three.

Jack climbed down the ladder and Jim followed. They coiled up the hose and Jack asked him questions about the RV. Was he going to wax the RV now? Would he take Jack for a ride? Could Jack sleep in it someday? Realizing these were important questions, Jim answered thoughtfully. There were many people who didn't "get" Jack. It warmed me watching the two together. Jim was unaware of Jack's diagnosis. He was not being kind out of pity. Their exchanges were genuine and organic. Jim accepted Jack as he was. He saw beyond Jack's impulsivity and lack of social boundaries. He saw the good in Jack.

I heard the door slam and heavy footprints trample into the kitchen where I was making a peanut butter and banana roll-up for Jack to eat for lunch. Ainsley was due any minute.

"Mom, I got paid! I am rich!" Jack yelled as he burst into the room.

"What?" I said, as I placed his meal on the table.

"Yup, Jim paid me," he said with such pride. He opened his hand to reveal four shiny quarters.

"I told him that a man should get paid for a day's work!" he said, as he waved his pointed finger at me with conviction.

"You're absolutely right, Jack. Now, sit down and eat your PB and banana."

He sat promptly, slapping his coins into the table, then lining them up two-by-two. I stood behind him, bent down and kissed his head. His hair was damp with a mixture of sweat and water. I paused slightly to drink him in. Slivers of hope poured in, from the reduced time and energy spent during his behavior in the van, to his positive interaction and attitude with Mr. Peters and, now, Jim. I could actually feel the shift happen. Jack was making steady strides and, on this day, I could see his sparkle was back again. He wasn't plagued by fear, overwhelmed, or desperately out of control. He had tools and used them. He self-regulated. He engaged with others.

Today, life was returning to Jack and me.

17

MARATHON TRAINING

*P*risms of sunshine filtered through the leafy trees, bathing the ground in speckled light, much like the colors in a kaleidoscope. I heard the rustle of the tall marsh grass sway as my path veered left. The tilt of sun created shadows as my feet pounded into the surface. The trail was spongy from the recent rain, allowing cool pockets to collect. It was September and a handful of leaves had begun to show their brilliance, marking a change. It was my fourth run that week. I preferred an early-morning run, but due to the rain I'd waited until after dinner and the kids were settled.

Although running was suggested to me by my therapist, I didn't surrender to the idea until after the meltdown. Not Jack's meltdown—mine. After a particularly dark day that followed a few great ones, I decided to try to perk myself up by singing a little car karaoke to one of my favorite songs. After pulling into the parking lot at the local supermarket, I broke down. Bent over the wheel, I wept wildly, held captive by the mess that crashed around in my head. I had been singing what had become my battle-cry song, Katy Perry's *Part of Me*.

The shame spiral was vicious and relentless. I loved my boy, but on days like this, filled with fear and doubt, my survival instinct kicked in. I felt an urgency to flee and I hated myself for it. How could I feel that way? How could I have those selfish thoughts about abandoning this child in trouble? What kind of a mother was I? I was a member of the freaking PTA who sold tickets at events and baked brownies for the bake sale. People knew me as having it all together. Well, I was clearly not together. I was unraveling...I heard a knock on the glass car window. It was a woman who I'd met years ago but had since lost touch with. I opened the door and fell into her arms.

As if I were being exorcised, I spewed out everything—how I wanted to leave and the pressure I felt of doing it right. The stress of it all was too much. The judgement I felt from others was compounded by the judgement I laid upon myself. The roller coaster that we had been on behaviorally was exhausting. Jack would have a few great days, then one horribly bad. I was spiritually bankrupt and couldn't remember the last time I felt true joy. My words flew out of my mouth so fast I couldn't have caught them if I had wanted to. She took her warm hands and cupped my face.

"Your therapist gave you permission to run. It might not be exactly the answer you were looking for, but the act of it is not only symbolic, but empowering. It's time to return some of your focus back to self-care. Remember the story about the oxygen masks? Before every lift-off, the flight attendant demonstrates aircraft safety and instructs that adults place the air mask on themselves before their children?"

I nodded. I knew where she was going, but also, I knew I desperately needed to hear it.

"If we don't take good care of ourselves, we can't be effective caretakers to those who need us. You have been filling Jack's cup, over and over and over again…now your cup is bone dry. No wonder you want to bolt out the door."

Tears flowed freely over my cheeks. She pulled me in with a mother's touch, wrapping around me like a well-worn quilt, her body soft and comforting. She held me with strong safe arms, not letting go for what seemed to be an eternity. I was embarrassed that I needed her, this virtual stranger, a woman who I recognized only by her face, seeing her in the audience of a meeting that I attended only on occasion. I didn't even know her name. As we released our embrace, she took my hands and faced me. She did not look uncomfortable or disgusted. Her eyes were not filled with judgement or fear. They were filled with love.

"Now, go buy a pair of running shoes!"

And so, I did. I went directly from the supermarket to the sporting goods store. It was clear to me that the universe had just tossed me a life-ring, and I trusted it would bring me back to my own shore.

TODAY WAS NOT AS INTENSE. We had come through some tough behaviors and seemed to be in a routine. The running and making space for myself anchored me in a way that I did not have before. If I wanted to, I could run this trail blindfolded. I knew each curve and dip, and where each trail led, and the unassuming location of wild blackberries, or ripened concord grapes dangling heavy on the vine. I smelled the sweetness of the grapes as I ran and allowed a wide smile to emerge. I felt my inner strength as my legs pumped and propelled me onward. At times, I was in the zone, not thinking —just moving my body at a rhythmic pace. Other times, thoughts came to visit. I sifted through them, sorting them into their place.

My mind drifted back to a day when I spoke with Jane. Ever since Jack had left school, I struggled with a sense of urgency to solve the situation. Even with Jack's positive momentum and a solid diagnosis of ASD, we faced professionals who were unsure how to create an environment that was the least restrictive as outlined by law, leaving his placement up in the air.

After I caught Jane up on Jack's home programming and therapy, I told her about his level of confusion about being home and not returning to school.

"I am worried that he will regress and that his behavior will amp up again," I said and then began to list the reasons why. Jane listened patiently.

"Nicole, this is a marathon, not a sprint," Jane said after a short pause. "Unfortunately, building a specialized program is not something that the district does easily. We have Bob Rafferty, who does not have special education background, and cannot grasp the complexities and needs of a child like Jack. He is used to having cookie-cutter programs that work for the majority of kids in the district. Jack is not cookie-cutter. He needs an individualized program in an inclusive setting."

"And that is the recommendation from Dr. Chambers.

Surely, it will help define and guide what they need to do for Jack," I said, hearing anxiety in my voice.

"Yes, while that is true, we are talking about the public-school district. Nothing moves fast. Especially when there's no formula to plug into. Thinking outside the box is a challenge. I am not trying to discourage you or diminish your feelings about the situation. I find it maddening too. What I am trying to do is to help you mentally prepare for the road ahead of us. This will be a race of endurance, not of speed."

My thoughts shifted to our August team meeting, and the tennis-match discussion that was spurred on by Dr. Chambers' report. Professionals, including Dr. Chambers, along with the district administration, attempted to integrate the information but struggled to find a ready-made solution. After a long pause, I heard Mr. Rafferty say for the umpteenth time, "this is a very unique situation," and Jane's words flooded into my brain.

This is a marathon. Not a sprint.

As I REACHED the last turn on the dirt path, I downshifted my body into a walking pace, stretched my arms up over my head, and then released them with a couple of shakes. My breath slowed, returning to a calm rhythm and my thoughts followed. Memories and feelings came and went, but I no longer had to run away. I believed running (as an activity) was part of my "marathon training," something to help me stay limber and strong. Just as essential were the ramblings that filled my journal. The act of freeing caged words—inadequacies and lies—to roam on the page lessened their power. I let the feelings and thoughts flow through me by way of my feet and my words.

I was rising up into a new light. I had a new understanding about control. I got to choose how any situation impacted me. I couldn't control the outcome of Jack's placement or if his behaviors spiked, but I could control how I held myself in the uncertainty. I got to decide whether I internalized other people's actions, words, or the situation as a whole. The power was within me.

18

TRUTH TELLING

I sat in Robin's waiting room. It was quiet, only the hum of the white noise machines vibrated through the air. Jack started to dig his hands into the building block basket and unknowingly splintered my silent bliss.

Jack saw Robin, his counselor, once a week. It took several months for him to talk about the events that occurred at the Bradford School. He refused to discuss what happed surrounding why he was no longer enrolled. He would say that he felt "normal" and that things were "normal." This was a kid who was not attending school due to his behaviors. Things were not fine, and his desire to ignore or deny blocked him from healing. We knew that the behaviors were a symptom of his diagnosis. He had become increasingly dysregulated, until finally his level of anxiety was heightened to a "flight or fight" response.

After Caroline had put the "stop light" regulation system in place and Maggie provided input for sensory calming tools, Robin was able to dive into the emotional components during their therapy sessions. Robin drew a boy figure on a piece of paper. She asked Jack to label how his body felt in relation to the red, yellow, and green system. If Jack was in "green," his head felt cool, but if he was in "red," his head felt hot. If Jack was in "green," his stomach was a little bit hungry, "yellow" he was really hungry and if he was in "red" he was not hungry at all. When he was in "green" his feet were jumpy, but in "red" they wanted to stomp. He also noted when he was in "red" his elbows felt sweaty.

After identifying the physical indicators of Jack's system, they were able to add the emotional pieces. When Jack was in "green," he described himself as happy. Jack drew a happy face next to the green circle on the stop light diagram he and Robin had sketched together. Next to the "yellow" circle, he drew an annoyed face, one with a straight mouth, and slanted eyebrows. Next to it he wrote, "Starting to get angry." On the "red" circle he penned an angry face and wrote, "Plain old mad." The illustrations, in connection with the physiological components, helped bridge the gap to the next step—the antecedent. Simply put, the antecedent is an event, action, or circumstance that happens before a behavior occurs.

Over several sessions, Robin and Jack worked on identifying his feelings in connection to a behavior or event. On a page titled "Plain old mad," Jack listed these reasons for his elevated state: Work too hard, can't find the words, when I'm being bossed around, when teacher is too close to my back, or when they pull a trick on me (like I think it is free time, but I am trapped in the study room). He made a page titled "Starting to get angry," and for yellow, identified he would begin to say mean things and sometimes argued or debated. On the last page, depicting green, it was titled: "Go with the flow." Listed in the description underneath was happy and feeling loose and cool.

These concrete illustrations enabled Jack to connect his actions (or reactions) to the feelings that spurred them on. He was beginning to label and recognize his feelings. He was beginning to see the correlation between how his body physically felt and his mood. The "stop light" procedure was systematically used across every setting of Jack's programming. It was born out of Jack's Behavior Intervention Plan, adapted from a lengthier regulation program that many therapists used. For it to be successful, everyone needed to be on the same page. Caroline was at the helm, checking in with Robin, Maggie, and me on a regular basis to monitor his progress and keep lines of communication clear.

"Look, Mom!" Jack shouted across the room and ran toward me, holding what appeared to be half of a tower structure.

"Wow!" I said, admiring at Jack's handiwork.

Robin's door opened and her smiling face appeared.

"Jack, I will be right out. See if you can build the other part of your tower while Robin and I catch up."

Jack sharply pivoted his body, walking back to the building materials, he plopped his body down with a thud. I went into Robin's office. It was part of the routine, to fill her in on anything noteworthy or of concern.

"I broke the news that he would not be going back to school with his brothers and friends, and that instead he would continue to be tutored at home."

"How did he take it?" Robin asked intently.

"He cried," I said, while my eyes filled up. "It broke my heart. It was the first time that he had expressed sadness about not attending school. Since then, he has mentioned it a few more times."

"Did he ask if he would go back to the Bradford School?" Robin asked

"He did, but I told him that I didn't know. He curled up on my lap and bawled."

"At the last team meeting, the school district was going to come up with a plan to bring him into one of the elementary schools for a peer social opportunity. Has the school district behaviorist been over to observe Jack?"

I updated her on the home visit status, which was almost non-existent. Jennifer Booth, the school district behaviorist, had visited on September 6th but not since. Caroline had recently attempted to connect with her, but they were now playing phone tag. Even Jane was trying to move things along, but it appeared Mrs. Booth's schedule was limited, and seeing Jack took effort. He wasn't visible in any of the three schools. She would have to make him a priority, which for whatever reason, she hadn't. The weekly home observations would definitely make the docket of ticket items to discuss at Jack's team meeting next week. We were already into October and I had expected the "lunch-bunch" group would be in motion by now. It was my understanding Mrs. Booth's visits were to assess Jack's readiness to go back into the school setting, and if she wasn't seeing him, how could she evaluate him?

"I know the waiting is frustrating, but it does give us time to prepare Jack and we know Jack doesn't like to be surprised. The more comfortable Jack is going in, the better." Robin said.

"True. And Caroline mentioned she wanted him to process

going back into an educational setting, so she has begun to prepare a social story to introduce the idea to Jack." I stated.

"That's perfect!" Robin said.

"I wonder if it's time?" I asked. Robin looked at me curiously.

"Time to tell him that he has Asperger's Syndrome? Maybe that it will enable him to understand himself better," I offered.

"Usually kids are a little bit older, but due to the circumstances, it could be a helpful for Jack, as he continues to process everything. He knows about his ADHD diagnosis. He likened his super-fast brain to a lightning bolt. Remember he did a drawing of it? How proud he was to be as smart as his big brother, who also has ADHD?" Robin had also treated Jack's older sibling.

I started to laugh because Jack's drawing was really a "stained glass" sun catcher made on a clear plastic twelve-inch square with special gel-paints for the design. He painted the background a deep blue, and the lightning bolt was large, silver, and right in the center. He obsessed about the placement of his masterpiece. He walked around with it, taking it to different rooms, placing it on every windowsill. He pointed to it and said, "This is my lightning bolt brain. Super-fast and super-smart!" This was followed by him dancing around as if he had just landed a touch-down pass in the super bowl. One of the lighter moments, before things exploded.

"I was just thinking about how happy Jack was after he made his lightning bolt. He liked being like his brother. I wonder how he'll take the news about his new diagnosis. Will it make him feel even more different?" I asked.

"That is a good point. But, the new information about being

on the spectrum won't erase the fact that he and his big brother have fast brains bursting with creative ideas. It will be an addition to what he already knows about himself."

We decide to tell Jack about his ASD diagnosis. A few days later, Jack and I sat on his bed and read a picture book called *What it is to Be Me! An Asperkid Book*, by Angela Wine. I liked the book because the illustrations and text are simple and direct. On the first page, Danny, the main character, introduced himself and told the reader he had Asperger's syndrome. Danny went on to describe things that he was good at and things that he struggled with, keeping a balance between both. Jack snuggled in with Gigi and I opened to the first page.

"Hi. My name is Danny. I have Asperger's Syndrome."

"What! ASS-BURGERS? This kid has burgers coming out of his ASS?" Jack shouted. Loud belly laughter erupted from his wiggly body.

"Ass-burgers…Ass-burgers…Ass-bur-gers!" He chanted, laughing so hard that he fell over and toppled off the twin bed. *This* was not going as I had imagined.

"Hi. I am Danny and I have burgers in my ass!" He announced, while holding his blanket on his bum, pretending it was hamburgers oozing out his bottom. He hooted at his own joke and then started to gallop around the room.

"Help my ass-burgers are chasing me!" His gait was awkward and rubbery. The cowlick on the left side of Jack's hairline was bouncing with him. Between the fall off the bed and the sweat of this work out it had broken free.

I sat on the bed trying not to crack a smile. This was funny. Horrifyingly funny. It was comical because, let's face it, Asperger's was an unfortunate name. Horrifying, because I had to reel him in and tell him that he too, was "afflicted" with *ass-burgers.*

After a few minutes of coaxing by pulling the trump card, I reminded Jack it was almost video game time, and that we needed to finish reading, he returned to the book. I pulled the weighted blanket over him, hoping it would work its magic, and provide grounding for his charged body.

I started reading, beginning with page two. We'd covered page one. Danny explained that he had sensitive ears, which were great for hearing, but loud noises bothered him (with a picture of Danny covering his ears with his hands, something that Jack did often). Danny mentioned that he was awesome at video games, but handwriting was hard for him. Sometimes, he didn't like to be touched, but he did like to be wrapped up tight in his blanket. Danny was friendly, but he had trouble with personal space. He was interested in how things worked and always asked lots of questions. Danny liked to talk about his favorite subjects but didn't notice when friends stopped listening. On one of the last pages, he told us he took what people said literally. Even if they were joking.

As the last page was read, Jack was quiet. He took the book and thumbed through the pictures. Minutes passed.

"Well, I am glad I don't have that! What time is it? Can I play my video games now?" he asked and tossed the book on the bed and moved toward the door.

"Ah, sure. It's after five o'clock," I said in a dream-like tone, feeling I just had an out-of-body experience.

He must have been able to identify with Danny, right? The sensitivity to sound, and how writing was a challenge, and no clue about personal space? The blanket! The freaking blanket?

Come on! Maybe he did and that was why he went into full denial mode.

The next day, I emailed Robin, and told her what had happened. To my surprise, she responded that this was not the first time she had heard "ass-burgers," making me feel slightly better. She recommended reading it again, but this time make the connections between Jack and Danny. That night, we sat down and I brought the book out.

"Not again!" he whined.

"Jack, I think this was a very interesting book and Robin asked for us to read it together."

"Fine. But it has silly pictures."

I ignored the comment and begin to read. I pointed out the commonalities between him and Danny after each page. At the end of the book there was a pause.

"I don't have ass-burgers, Mother," Jack said in a snarky tone.

"Well, actually, you do. Remember when you went to see Dr. Chambers, the woman with the long hair and the office with the egg-shaped chairs?"

"Yeah, those chairs were cool."

"Well, she did all kinds of tests while you were there trying to figure out why you were having a hard time in school. She discovered that you are on the autism spectrum. That you have Asperger's Syndrome, like Danny."

He was silent.

"Your body has a hard time processing sight, sound, smells, tastes, and touch. You have a hard time mechanically processing the ideas that originate in your brain to come out through your hand, that's why writing is a challenge and you don't like doing it. You struggle with self-regulation—and react to the environment or situations. Your emotions become so big that you lose control. This is what happened to you at school and now sometimes at home."

Jack sat quietly and looked down at the Lego guy in his lap. He twisted the guy's head back and forth.

"Because they didn't know, because we didn't know you had Asperger's, the school was not giving you the support you needed. You weren't given the opportunity to be in a program that would have taught you skills to navigate a typical education classroom. They did not treat your autism; they disciplined your behavior. Kids with autism, or Asperger's, are more successful with having specific educational and social instruction that is tailor-made for them."

There was a long pause. I know I have just used way too many words. It was essentially the equivalent of throwing a bucket of bouncy balls and seeing how many he could catch. It was not fair. Not fair for him to have to learn that he "has" something else.

"You know, Jack, there are a lot of awesome things about Asperger's Syndrome. Many people who have autism have photographic memories. Their brain remembers what they see— exactly—as if they took a photo of it and stored it inside their head. Just like you and the books you read. Why do you think we have to get so many books each week?"

He looked at me with curious eyes.

"Because, my tutors make me read all the time!" he blurted out indignantly.

"Well, that may be true, they do want you to read all the time, but more importantly, we have to get lots of books because we discovered that you were not reading the words, you had memorized them. Your brain was able to read through it once and remember it so well that you tricked us!"

Jack's gaze was reaching beyond me as if he was somewhere else. His mouth cracked a smile. Was he remembering all the times he "read" *Captain Underpants*?

"You also have amazing visual spatial skills. You can assimilate in your mind how things fit together. That is why you are so good at puzzles and building with Legos."

He nodded as if he already knew that.

"You are also outgoing and will make friends everywhere you go. Not everyone can do this! How lucky you are to be able to meet someone new and ask them to play."

I had found it interesting after Jack was diagnosed with autism, being outgoing—overly outgoing—was part of his disability. Because Jack was social, I thought he couldn't be autistic. I had been led to believe children with autism had difficulty communicating. While it was classified as a communication disorder, I never thought about the flip side. Kids with high-functioning autism may be extremely social, but have difficulty reading social cues. We had recently become aware that as Jack aged, being the "mayor" was less acceptable by his peers, especially when he was not cluing into their body language or taking their perspectives during cooperative play.

Jack took the Lego guy and placed it into my hand.

"Are we done here?" he asked, his voice tight. "Because, it is video game time!"

And off he ran...

19

GIGI'S SUPER SAFETY PLAN

*W*e finally received the phone call from Caroline regarding, "Lunch Bunch," a new group for Jack. He had done well with Maggie, his OT, and another peer in her clinic, so Caroline pushed for second opportunity for Jack. Lunch Bunch would be held at the Webster School once a week during lunch. Jack would meet with the school social worker and a student peer and the three would eat together. She told me she had been in contact with Mrs. Booth, the school district behaviorist, to coordinate weekly home visits, as was discussed at the meeting. Mr. Rafferty made it clear that Mrs. Booth would be more involved moving forward. He wanted Jack and our family to become familiar with her, with the understanding there would be a transition from Caroline and Atlas Educational staff to the school district staff once Jack was acclimated back into our public school system.

"Mr. Rafferty liked the idea of Jack beginning his transition back to into school with OT services first instead of Lunch Bunch. It was recommended instead of it being one-to-one instruction it would be in an OT group, but when Mrs. Booth spoke to the school OT, she said it would be difficult to find peers," Caroline explained. "And to be quite honest, to start with OT would be a mistake. Writing is hard for Jack. If the OT places demands on him, especially writing demands and in front of peers? That could set him off."

I nodded silently while I took copious notes as if Caroline could view me through the phone.

"After a few rounds and a few other ideas, we came full circle. Lunch Bunch is confirmed to be his first transition back into the public-school setting. He will begin next week with Joy Damon at the Webster School. She is the social worker who will be running the program with Jack and one other student. He will go every Wednesday and have lunch in a separate room from the cafeteria with a peer his age and Mrs. Damon."

I was ecstatic to hear Jack was finally moving back into school. He was doing really well, between the therapies and the anti-anxiety medication, so I had hopes this would be a solid jumping off place for him. He had been receptive to the social story Caroline had scripted, as well as the work he and Robin had been doing to get ready. I felt reassured to hear Joy Damon would be involved, as she was not only the social worker at the Webster School but worked closely with Robin, Jack's counselor. Robin had mentioned her as someone she thought would be a good fit for Jack within the school district.

"Having lunch and chatting with another peer? Jack will love it!" I said.

"It is a steppingstone and depending how he does behaviorally, more opportunities will be added."

"But…wait. Who will be with him? At school? Will it be Ainsley? What will happen if he goes into red?" My excitement had morphed into panic.

"All good questions! Yes, Ainsley will be with Jack the whole time. If he does become agitated and needs to take a break, the other child will be removed, and Jack will be directed to take a break with his calming materials. Ainsley will use the BIP, just like we do in your home, but in the school setting."

"Okay, that makes me feel better." I exhaled. My shoulders relaxed a bit as she reassured me of the plan.

"Jack has been building up his time sitting and being attentive during table instruction and work. Being 'table-ready' is part of the criteria for moving back into a school setting. The other one may be a bit harder for him to achieve…It's something we need to talk about and put into action as soon as possible."

Oh, no. What was she going to tell me?

"Okay?" I said in quieter voice than anticipated.

"We need a plan for Gigi."

"You mean his blanket?"

"Yes, his blanket. To him, Gigi, is more than just a blanket. Gigi is real," Caroline paused, allowing the words to hang in the air. "Gigi has been Jack's security, his friend, his confidant, for many months. Gigi has a persona. Leaving his safety object behind could be a trigger moving forward. He is so attached to Gigi, that not having him at his disposal, to help him calm or feel centered, could set him off."

I hated to admit it, but she was right. Since Jack left school, he had become extremely attached to his childhood baby blanket. He had conversations with him, carried him around the house, and even brought him to his therapy sessions. I say "he" because Jack firmly corrected me one day when I mistakenly called it a "her." And if I called him an "it," well, I got the same reaction, with the addition of bulging eyeballs and clenched fist, albeit trying to hide the small smirk that was underneath, but clearly showing me that he was offended by my insensitivity. Truly, with all of his heart, he thought of Gigi as a friend.

Months ago, in the aftermath of the escape from school, I would ask him why he ran away. His answer was that he wanted to come home and see me. But, when I pressed him further, asking him why, he responded, "That's between me and Gigi," and he clammed up.

"This—leaving Gigi behind—will be *really* hard for him. I'm afraid, that he will have red behaviors, possibly another extinction burst." I said reluctantly.

"I am not going to lie to you, Nicole. He probably will go through another extinction burst," Caroline responded in a measured calm tone.

Panic vibrated through me.

I couldn't fathom going back to that place. It was only a few months ago, the days of dodging flying objects and chairs, pounding fists and pulling hair. The days of constant worry, waiting for the land mines to ignite, for him to push back —*hard*.

"But I have a plan. A super safety plan for Gigi. I am working on a social story that outlines protocol for keeping Gigi safe from harm's way. I am banking on the belief if the story is energetic and is focused on Gigi's well-being, he might buy into it," she said in a cautiously optimistic tone.

Caroline continued to describe the social story and the reward system she would be putting in place, called the "Super Safety Plan for the Incredible Gigi." The plan called for two "fortresses," or beds, Gigi would go into at specific times. The purpose of the plan was to "protect Gigi from accidental loss or harm" by placing him in "secret lock-down mode" when Jack was either working with his tutors or leaving the house. Jack had (unknowingly) decorated two shoe boxes (fortresses) in preparation for the plan—one to be left at the front door and one just outside of the study room.

The reward system was called "The Super Safe Gigi Goal," and it outlined the criteria and the number of "stars" Jack would need to earn to choose a prize. Jack could earn stickers but had to put Gigi in his fortress when asked and stay in the yellow or green during the activity. Caroline said that Jill would be coming in tomorrow with the new social story and a huge bag of toys. She mentioned something about Jill looking like the female version of Kris Kringle.

"The plan will begin tomorrow," Caroline said, making sure we were on the same page.

I took a deep breath and channeled my best version of being cautiously optimistic and hung up the phone. This was what I wanted. To move forward. To have him with typical peers. I didn't want my nerves to overrun the good things that were happening... *These were good things.*

Caroline and her staff had earned my trust, which was not something I gave blindly anymore. I was still recovering from the heartache of the situation and how specific things were handled with Jack by professionals. Even with the best intentions, it caused him harm. But, how could we see if Jack was truly ready for the next step if we didn't push him? It was our job to prepare him for the future by stretching his boundaries. If we played it safe, how would that benefit him?

My fear came from the dark places we had traveled to in recent months. The memories, still raw, swirled inside of my stomach, revisiting me and bringing a sour taste to my mouth. I leaned my head back into the couch cushion and closed my eyes. I could feel my heart beating, slow and steady. A gust of sweet Indian summer air rushed through the open slider, washing over me like a prayer. I heard Ainsley and Jack upstairs. It sounded like cleaning up, as she directed him, "put those pieces here, and grab the lid for the box," and I heard his kinetic body move over the floorboards above me.

"Now, it's Jack's choice! You get to decide what we do next!" Ainsley announced loudly.

When I heard Jack choosing his next activity, it reminded me of a precious truth: I could choose, too. I got to choose how I framed the next phase of Jack's programming. It could be filled with fear, projecting all the things that could happen, all the numerous ways it could go sideways…or I could trust.

Although Caroline had remained quiet during the summer months, focused on recovering from a health issue, she was in contact with us, the district, and his service providers. During those turbulent summer months, I was frustrated and fearful. I often felt that we were in free-fall, but what I didn't recognize was that we were deep within the process of the plan she had penned prior to her medical leave. Even if she was available to put my fears at bay, it would have not changed how the plan set things in motion. The behaviors and the reshaping…It took as long as it took.

And now, he was beginning to rise. I could see it in his body language, it had begun to soften. I could hear it in his voice and the occasional laughter that exploded from his mouth when he was playing with his tutor. I could feel it when he sat next to me, leaning in, like he used to. I could read it in his data, the visual documentation that his behaviors were on a decline. The evidence was all around me. Making the connection between what I *knew* and what I *felt* was the challenge. It was also a process. Spiraling into the "what-if's" was counterproductive and having a kid who was sensitive to energy, well, to think he wouldn't feel the vibe I'd be throwing out was naïve.

It was time to get real with my fears, sit with them and let them go, allowing for time and creating space to heal myself. I'd asked Jack to trust. He had new people coming into his life, new rules and expectations, and he was walking through his fears, processing them, and getting beyond his former experiences. If he could be brave, then so could I.

Mentally, I committed to spending time with my journal, to explore the layer that had surfaced. It was the only way I could see to get beyond the fear. The only way to get beyond it was to go through it.

———

"It's Lunch Bunch day!" Jack sang.

"Yes, it is. Are you excited to go to school? Meet a new friend?" I asked, attempting to take a temperature read prior to going into the school building.

"Yup!" I wonder if it will be a boy or a girl!" he said, tapping his pointer finger to his chin thoughtfully.

"I believe it will be a boy your age. Here, let's pack your lunch. We need to get ready," I said, moving into the kitchen. "We will meet Ainsley there, too. And a new teacher. Do you remember her name?" I asked, wondering if he retained the information that we had been spooning him.

"Yes…Mrs. Darwin?"

I let out a laugh.

"Well, close. It's Mrs. Damon. She is very nice. And, she knows Robin!" I said, knowing it would give her street cred, as Jack loved Robin.

"Whoop-whoop!" Jack exclaimed and ran to the door.

When we arrived at the Webster School, I was edgy. I didn't anticipate how I would feel; it was all about getting Jack prepared. We even listened to classical music on the way over trying to keep the mood light. We met Ainsley at the front of the building. As we stepped into the office, a woman greeted us with an enormous smile. She was slim and petite. Her blond hair brushed the tops of her shoulders.

"Hi Jack! My name is Mrs. Damon!" She held out her hand for him to shake it.

Jack awkwardly took her hand. His gaze was fixated on her grip.

"Are you ready to go meet Timmy for Lunch Bunch?" Her eyes sparkled with enthusiasm.

"Ready!" he exclaimed loudly.

As I watched them walk away, I felt a pang inside my chest. I looked around. I was alone, standing in the open two-story foyer. There were two benches on either side of the office door. I chose one and sat down. Twenty-five minutes. It was only twenty-five minutes. He could hold it together for that long, right? I felt the fear bubble, just below the surface. Although I was completely comfortable with Ainsley, and Joy Damon came highly recommended, I didn't know how Jack was going to react. And no matter how much planning and preparation had gone into this day, it was still reentry. As I sat on the hard wooden bench, I realized, once again, the outcome was out of my control. It was the first time in many months he was in other people's care in a public-school setting. I also realized that having a panic attack right outside of the school office would not be ideal. I focused on my breath and tried to distract myself by watching the coming and goings of the busy foyer.

A mother and young child came into the front doors holding hands; school staff walked past me; and a janitor moved swiftly down the hall pushing a dust broom. I felt their eyes on me. It was probably my imagination. I was in a sensitive state, sitting out in the open, and felt a bit vulnerable. I looked for a different diversion, so I pulled out my phone. I scrolled down my Facebook feed and saw posts from friends and family of fun outings, pictures of their smiling kids, and the celebratory gushing of team victories from the night before. It struck me as funny how my priorities had shifted. My gauge for success, and certainly Jack's success, was not about winning a soccer game any longer.

Several minutes later, I saw Jack and Mrs. Damon walking toward me. Ainsley followed closely behind. He was smiley, but bouncy. I caught Ainsley 's eye and she gave me a nod, affirming that he was okay.

"He did great!" Mrs. Damon said as she reached me.

"Oh, I'm so glad!"

"Okay, Jack, I will see you next week!" she said cheerfully.

Jack began to walk toward the front door, and then he turned back.

"Don't forget to bring the UNO game for our ride in the elevator!" he yelled.

20

A MATTER OF TRUST

I watched Jill and Jack pass through the family room while unspooling a roll of toilet paper. His steps were deliberate and controlled, attempting to not tear the paper. His face a mask of concentration, he stopped abruptly and doled out a few more feet before he rounded the corner.

"Good remembering, Jack! That's right, so it's not too snug," Jill said encouragingly.

I sat on the couch surrounded by months of team meeting documents, printed emails and handwritten notes detailing phone conversations between Caroline, Jane, and Mr. Rafferty. I was swimming in paperwork and happy to have a curious distraction.

"This will demonstrate how many miles the sun is from Earth and the other planets," Jill said, after seeing my bewildered look.

"And we've got earth right here!" Jack announced, pointing to a circular hand-colored planet that Jill was holding.

Jack's tutors had woven science activities into his programming, which incorporated movement. These opportunities kept his interest while he was academically learning. He was able to attend because it was fun and acknowledged Jack's need for movement. Jack, at his core, was a kinetic kid, and movement helped Jack regulate, enabling him to focus on other areas of his academics. Jack had increased his time sitting for table instruction and having opportunities for movement was necessary for him to remain in control. Last week, after his tutor decided that the yoga ball in his study room was too stimulating, Jack, trying to be helpful, sent it bouncing down the staircase to the first floor. He laughed, watching it bounce, until it reached the landing, and knocked the pendulum clock off the wall. It fell to the wood floor below with a violent crash. The glass face of the clock smashed, and Jack quickly covered his ears at the top of the steps. He ran back into the study room and hid in his pop-tent. A few months ago, the incident of the crashing clock would have taken him longer for to regain composure. His compulsive nature required opportunities for motor breaks, and guidance of when to take them, but he'd come a long way from where he started. Before he had access to calming tools (tent, safe space, sensory box), he might have escalated from an overstimulated yellow into a red zone, producing destructive behavior.

I had a conference call that afternoon with Jane and Mike to prepare for the next team meeting. I scanned through the recent notes of conversations, observations, and data compiled over the course of the last team meeting. Jane would want an update from his time at home and his progress with the service providers. Gathering, sorting and reviewing these materials were essential for building a case for Jack's current abilities and needs. Not wanting to forget anything, I jotted down bullet points and was armed with sticky notes to flag pages of importance.

Administratively, things were moving slowly even though Jack had been responding well to the behavior plan, the discreet trials, and therapies. Mike and I continued to push. At the late October meeting, Joy Damon reported how well Jack had been doing in Lunch Bunch. When there was discussions suggesting another component be added to his programming at the Webster school, Mr. Rafferty declared that he was not going to "build a program" at the Webster School and that the Bradford School had all the supports Jack would need, being a child on the autism spectrum. The Burbridge School district had an autism program located at the Bradford School. Any young child that received services for autism, no matter what their "home" school was, was transported and attended the Bradford School. Because of the location base, Rafferty's logic was Jack should return there. As the discussion circulated around the table, we were asked to bring Jack into the Bradford School to observe how he would react to being inside the building. Even though I didn't want to agree, I knew we were continuing to build a case, ultimately keeping the big picture of what was most beneficial for Jack's educational and emotional/social needs. Honestly, I wasn't sure if Rafferty was bluffing. He didn't think we would do it, and it would give him leverage to suggest another program, landing Jack outside of the district. There was a game and a dance to these negotiations. We only had Jack to think about; Rafferty had a whole district.

A visit to the school was an interesting concept for a few reasons. As Jack's parents, we felt that returning to Bradford wasn't the best placement for him given the staff's prior mishandling of him and failure to identify (or communicate to us) that Jack was a child who exhibited autistic tendencies. If the visit went well and they recommended he return, so many questions and details would need to be hashed out, due to his history. But, having been identified with a diagnosis of autism, maybe it would be different? Who would be working with him? Surely, it could not be the current school social worker or the vice principal who had been so ill-equipped to handle or understand Jack's previous cries for help.

At the November team meeting, Bradford's principal announced that there was "no room for Jack" at their school, citing that it was an old building and she was unable to carve out a room exclusively for Jack's programming. This revelation was mentioned a few minutes into the meeting, after I gave my account of the three visits I had made with Jack to the school. What was more cutting was the principal's admission of reviewing the building blueprint right after the October meeting; this meant she had known for weeks.

I was furious! They had all month to tell us, to let us know that a Bradford placement was "off the table," but chose not to. Instead they waited, while I found excuses to bring Jack into the school. It was irresponsible and cruel. Jack handled each outing well, only hiding behind me a couple of times when other adults passed us in the hallway. Of course, his mood was slightly elevated; he was walking back into the building he ran from. How did the principal keep this information under her hat while I traipsed him around her building? She knew I was there. She arranged a time for Jack to go the school library during non-classroom hours. Were they buying time, waiting for Jack to fail?

It was hard not to take this personally, particularly during our interactions with the school librarian who shouted from across the room not to touch any books in the section where Jack and I stood. She gave us a quick and dirty tour of the area of age-appropriate books for Jack. Her annoyance level persisted at the check-out desk as she made a point to remind Jack about the return policy with a stern tone. The vibe she was throwing down was that she anticipated a problem from him. To my knowledge, Jack enjoyed going to the library at school and it was never an issue. No outstanding fees. No behavior problems. He loved books, way back to his days with Mr. Peters and preschool story hour, but this librarian was no Mr. Peters. To be honest, I wanted to punch her. It infuriated me, not only people assuming he was going to be a problem, but that *he was the problem.*

She wasn't the only person we'd experienced such dismissive behavior from. She was one on a list of many who barely knew Jack, only what they heard about him. These judgements were harmful. I saw them and felt them. If you think for a moment that Jack didn't feel her discontentment—her negativity—think again. Kids on the autism spectrum are super sensitive beings. I saw the way he looked at her as she scanned his books. The tightness across his shoulders. The smile faded from his lips when she tersely said, "no, you can't use the wand to check the books out. That's my job."

After our dissatisfied reaction to the announcement of the Bradford School being off the table during the meeting, our advocate pushed for more time at the Webster School. Joy Damon reported Jack had continued success and recommended that another social opportunity be added. She was becoming a good advocate for Jack, always having something positive to say about him. It was determined that the two behaviorists, Caroline and Jennifer Booth, would collaborate on a plan for transition, adding another Lunch Bunch (two times a week) and recess. In preparation, Jennifer interviewed Jack's past school specials teachers (gym, music, art), and reported Jack was never a problem in their classes. The transition plan would systematically outline opportunities for inclusion during these classes, adding one at a time using behavioral criteria as their guide for admittance. The data would drive Jack's transition. This was essential, since the behavior plan was the cornerstone to Jack's programming.

"Did you talk to Mae Paulson about this?" Jane asked Mr. Rafferty at the meeting.

"No, I have not spoken to Mrs. Paulson yet," he said.

"Well, she will need to approve Jack moving to the Webster School. She is the principal—she has the final say." Jane paused, looking to Mr. Rafferty for an answer.

"She has to take him. Now, let's move on…" He said, shuffling through papers splayed out in front of him.

Jane leaned over and whispered to Mike and me noting that Mae was a bit of a hard-ass and was not going to like being put in this position.

Over the next month, while Caroline and Jennifer Booth collaborated on Jack's transition plan, and Atlas staff schedules were adjusted to accommodate the proposed changes involving his time between home and school, Mae Paulson put her foot down. There would be no further transition until she met with Mr. Rafferty, and she was not available to meet with him for at least another week. Jack was suspended in mid-air, once again. We were on hold waiting for this meeting to happen to determine if she would allow this transition to continue at the Webster School.

At the December team meeting held at the Webster School, Rafferty publicly apologized for speaking for Mrs. Paulson at the last meeting. He continued by saying how grateful he was that Mrs. Paulson had agreed to oversee Jack's transition into the Webster School. Discussions surrounding grade placement surfaced. As a returning student, would second be the appropriate grade? His past behavior had impacted learning the first-grade curriculum, and he was struggling to catch up. Caroline Chase, in addition to being a BCBA, was also an educator and had concerns about Jack's phonemic awareness. He was reading below grade level and writing continued to be a trigger. Beyond academics, socially Jack would fit better in a younger class. His social deficits would make it more challenging. He needed to learn social skills and, by going down a grade, this would allow him time. Overall, the team was concerned that if we assigned him to second grade it could be setting him up for failure.

After some debate, it was determined that Jack would be enrolled as a first-grade student at the Webster School, beginning January 1, 2013. Robin began to lay down the foundation for Jack to accept his first-grade status. We anticipated it would be a blow to him emotionally. Mrs. Damon was looking for a first-grade peer to be added to Lunch Bunch to ensure Jack would know someone in his class. In addition to finding another peer, Mrs. Damon, who was the CPI (crisis prevention) trainer for staff in the district, set up a training session for those who would be working with Jack. Caroline suggested Jack have a round of academic testing to determine any additional deficits, specifically in regard to his phonemic awareness. When Jack's neuropsychological testing was administered by Dr. Chambers the prior June, she was unable to test him in this area due to his tolerance level. The team agreed that academic testing should be done, but after the transition.

During those three months of coordination prior to the announcement of Jack becoming an official Webster student, the leg work was sizable and strenuous. The day-to-day logistics of transporting him to therapy appointments, over to the school and back to the house for tutoring was one thing, but the transition plan, with all its intricacies, was an entirely different animal.

Although, we were all working together for the same common goal (to get Jack educated), we were divided at times. There was an "us vs. the establishment" undercurrent. Even though we were all "Team JD," we didn't work to the same end. The non-public school providers had a vision of building an individualized program for Jack, but their vision didn't fit intuitively into the existing public-school model. Early on, we, as his parents, had to determine which provider was in the lead within the inner circle of Jack's support team. Atlas Educational Services had been contracted by the school district to deliver home services and, with Caroline Chase at the helm, she provided the most effective approach for Jack. As an educator and Board Certified Behavior Analyst (BCBA), she had expertise in dual areas. Her systematic approach to treating his behavior and keen awareness to his antecedents had enabled Jack to find regulation again, thus allowing him to access his academics once more. We deferred to Caroline and asked the team to do so as well.

Defining who was in the driver's seat was an effective way to keep his programming on track. As Jack was transitioned into the school setting, we had a new principal and other teaching and therapeutic staff join his team. The principal, Mae Paulson, was in charge of the Webster School and her staff. Mr. Rafferty had requested Mrs. Paulson's cooperation and for her to work with Caroline, but as the transition into the Webster School got under way, a power struggle emerged.

We were asking the district to create an individualized educational program. The goal was for Jack to be fully integrated into a regular education classroom while having access to therapeutic and academic supports, thus enabling him to reach his highest potential. Caroline was diligent and could anticipate holes in the plan before they surfaced. The district, which in the past took a reactive, not proactive approach, thought she was a bit like "Henny Penny," projecting outcomes before they happened. Proactive vs. reactive. As his parents we preferred a proactive approach, as Jack had already proven at the Bradford School that a reactive protocol wasn't effective. We pressed to have Caroline in the forefront of Jack's programming to ensure for carryover and consistency.

What was challenging for me was recognizing and quieting the fear-based scenarios of Jack's recent past. The act of leaving Jack in the building and not camping out on the bench in front of the main door was a big step. It was physically and emotionally draining to hand him off for Lunch Bunch and recess and walk away. When fierce maternal instincts surfaced, I became wound up in the tendrils of past trauma and memories. Unconsciously, I thought that if I was near him, he would be okay.

I was struggling with trusting people in his life, even family. I would step in and undermine Mike when he was parenting Jack if I thought he was not following the plan. God forbid anyone tried to discipline him or say something that would be harmful... watch out! He had been wounded, and because of that, I was on high alert.

Fueling my apprehension was the feedback I received about Jack's sessions at the school. A variety of concerns surfaced. The first one was when Mrs. Damon let Jack ride the elevator to the second floor every day before Lunch Bunch. Caroline and Ainsley were concerned it gave Jack too much control in his new setting. It was potentially problematic as Jack had shown a fascination with the elevator ride and breaking the pattern could be challenging. One of Jack's goals on his IEP was to learn to walk in the hall appropriately. Typically, the elevator was only permitted for children (or staff) who had a physical limitation. Allowing Jack to use the elevator was not modeling behavior as outlined in his Individualized Education Plan (IEP). Moreover, it might have given him the inclination that he didn't have to play by the rules.

The peer Jack had been paired with for Lunch Bunch was very accommodating. He deferred to Jack in all areas. The peer was working on becoming more assertive, but Jack got to revive his role as "mayor," making it easy for him to assume control. The dynamic was identified, and another peer was to be added. The elevator use and peer interaction could become a catapult for future behaviors. Every part of Jack's transition needed to be keenly examined so we didn't end up where we were last March.

Caroline was the point person between her staff and Webster personnel. When she found out that another student was using Jack's subset room (a room dedicated for Jack to deescalate) during the time that he was in there, she questioned what would happen if Jack had a behavior and this other student was in room? How would it be handled? When recess was added to the lunch block, concerns about him being outside and the possibility of escape appeared. Caroline worked with staff to trouble shoot how to make it safe for him to be included. She was a master at teasing out the finer details, of seeing red flags before things spun out of control, and she understood Jack.

Caroline understood what he was capable of. She knew how his brain worked. She had spent the past several months collecting Jack's data, extinguishing maladaptive behaviors, and shaping new, more positive ones. She was a Jack expert. Now she had to teach new staff how to be Jack experts, too. This would take time. I was acutely aware that the clock was ticking. The district would pull Atlas services out of the school once Jack had completed the transition. I knew the school behaviorist, Jennifer, was spread thin and I was leery of the time she had to dedicate to Jack's case. The lack of attentiveness when she was slated to conduct home visits wasn't due to the lack of desire or understanding, it was because she was already over scheduled.

Who would be at the helm when Caroline and Atlas were gone? This was a real fear that came knocking often. My fears were continuously being fed by our diligence, the anticipation of what could happen, and the experience of what did happen. The circular motion was hard to break free from as we embarked on the journey back into the public school. We were forging a new path for Jack and pushing boundaries within the school system and within ourselves. The stakes were high, and we knew it.

A few weeks into Jack's new schedule I had another panic attack. It brought me to my knees. I had been on spin cycle for far too long, caught up again in the drama of what could happen. Being proactive was good but allowing it to consume me was costly. I amped up my self-care routines, journaling, and meeting with Janet or friends when I could. It was a roller-coaster ride where panic and hope were within seconds of each other. I needed to be kind and patient with myself during this period of unknowns.

Weeks turned into months and we persisted. Jack was taking things in stride at school with only a few incidents that were ironed out swiftly. More and more, I was using my voice. I was no longer held down by the negative undertow of thoughts and spoke up when I felt concerns bubble up inside of me. I had never thought of myself as someone who did not use her voice, but trauma doesn't play by the rules. Trauma takes our voice, our will, and our power away. Trauma suffocates.

The panic attacks forced me to address the past while helping me look forward. Replacing fear-based thoughts, the ones that spun inside my head, with positive ones brought a change in my perspective. In accessing this new tool, along with using other self-care practices, I felt lighter. Like spring after a long winter, I was hopeful and emerging. I could see glimpses of a new life and day by day I was learning how to trust myself to navigate the new landscape. I could do this.

21

YOU'LL SHOOT YOUR EYE OUT!

I heard the squeak of the dial turn and the rush of water flow out of the faucet; the rhythm of dancing feet jived on the hard tile floor above me, making the light fixture vibrate. A few seconds passed, the rumbling subsided, and I wondered if he got into the tub. *Slam.* Nope. It was the sound of the toilet lid smashing onto the porcelain bowl, I'd recognize that sound anywhere, even if it was rarely followed by the sound of a flush. Jack hardly ever flushed. He was always going way too fast to pause, stop, and flush.

The smooth sound of casters rolled on the metal track above me. It signaled the glass door of the tub was open and he was moving towards getting clean.

"Mom... I'm going in!" exclaimed Jack, followed by a splash and a thud.

"Are you okay, buddy?" I shouted from the bottom of the stairwell, not really worried, loud and abrupt was how he moved from point A to point B.

"I'm fine!" he yelled over the roar of water.

I grabbed the laundry basket brimming with clean, unfolded clothes and ascended the stairs. Once I arrived at the top, I peered into the bathroom and saw Jack's shadowy figure behind the frosted glass doors, confirming that he was, in fact, in the tub. I heard the hurried water pour out from the spigot, warm mist rising above the glass doors, and saw the accumulation of fog lingering on the top of the massive mirror that hung over the double sinks.

I turned into my bedroom and placed basket on our bed and started the folding process. I have four kids and one husband. Laundry was never ending. I pulled out a pair of blue jeans from the basket and held them up to assess who they belonged to... Patrick? After a minute or two, the water stopped, and I could hear the two older boys downstairs talking about the hottest and latest Xbox game slated for release. Jack's sing-song voice chimed in, rising above the glass enclosure, and echoed into the upstairs foyer. His jibber-jabber included the names of Kirby and King Dedede; no doubt he was recreating a scene from memory.

I brought the folded towels into the bathroom and placed them in the linen closet. Jack chattered away with no acknowledgement I had come into the room. I quietly slid the glass door open to check on him or, more precisely, the water level. Jack's love for water had been documented by the stain on our kitchen ceiling. Jack accidentally flooded the newly renovated upstairs bathroom six months ago. He forgot to shut the water off after he brushed his teeth one morning. It overflowed, seeping into the floor, into the kitchen and the basement below. He was taking too long, so I called for him as we were in danger of missing the school bus—*again*. I imagined he was playing in the sink and upon hearing my urgent plea to "not have a repeat performance of chasing bus 17 down the street," he came running. I had to admit, I would have moved too. I was yelling and having a fit about missing the bus, which in hindsight, seemed minute.

"Hi Mom," Jack said, while he moved his hands sharply in an awkward motion. His legs were crossed and both hands were placed precariously over his private area. I paused and looked at him.

"Jack, are you okay? Is something going on down there that I need to look at?" I asked. I thought maybe he had a rash or a patch of dry skin.

"Uh, no. I'm fine," he said refusing to look at me. He grimaced and placed his left hand on the glass door trying to slide it closed.

"Wait a minute," I said as I placed my hand flatly on the door. "You're acting funny, Jack. I am sorry, but I need to see what's going on down there to make sure you're all right," I said as I tried to catch his eyes.

Jack shrugged and slowly moved his hands away from his groin. At first glance, I thought he had an erection, which happens with young boys his age and it can feel weird and uncomfortable, so it made sense that he would try to hide it from me, feeling embarrassed. But, as I peered down at it, I could see it was oddly pressed against his lower abdomen, making it stand straight up. Oddest erection I'd ever seen. There was a lack of buoyancy, no freedom of movement—like it was cemented in place.

"See, its fine!" he said loudly.

"Can you stand up for a minute? I need to get a better look," I asked him casually, as I tried to downplay the situation.

"But… I will be cold if I stand up!" he said in a whining tone, he pushed back.

"Just for a minute," I promised.

He stood up. I looked at his penis, still upright, pasted against his boyish figure—glued! *Super glued!* I instantly remembered Jack and Ainsley had used super glue on a snow globe project. She asked me for this ultra-strong-bonding glue to repair the center piece that had broken off. I'd forgotten to grab it out of the tutoring room to put it away out of reach.

"Jack, did you use super glue on your penis?" I asked, knowing the truth already, hoping I was wrong.

"Yes, I did. I dared myself to do it!" he conceded.

"What? Why would you dare yourself to put super glue on your body?" I asked, noticing dried crusty streaks of superglue streaming down his left leg.

"I don't know! Sometimes… I just do that," he said exasperated. "I'm cold! Can I sit down now?"

Oh. My. God. How in the world do you get super glue off of that area? Was I going to have to take him the ER and explain to them how my autistic son decided to glue his penis to his belly? Oh, I hated the idea of trying to explain this to the ER staff. Would they understand that it stemmed from his diagnosis?

I felt a twinge shoot up from my spine to the base of my skull.

"Mom! Can I sit down now?" he asked again.

"Yes, you can sit for a minute," I said. My brain was in overdrive. I searched for options. He placed his hand on the door and tried to slide it closed.

"Jack, stop. I need to figure this out. I need to get this off of you. I don't know how to remove super glue. I may have to take you to the hospital and have a doctor remove it!"

"WHAT? I am NOT going to the hospital! They give shots at the hospital and I am NOT going there!" His voice was filled with fear. The situation was spiraling. I had to reel it in. I could do this. I mean, this has happened to someone else before, right? Glue on skin?

Getting up from the tile floor, I saw the empty tube of glue lying on top of the trash. I fished out the box. I scanned the box and in small letters it read: *If fingertips become glued together during application, remove glue with vegetable oil.* Vegetable oil. Good. I have that! In a flash, I felt relieved this could be handled at home. Probably no ER today. I stood with my hands holding the box and I caught my reflection in the large bathroom mirror. My hair was pulled back in a clip, face white-washed with worry, and I was dressed in my favorite tattered grey 2006 Disney sweatshirt.

It dawned on me how totally ridiculous this was. My son had glued his penis to his belly with super glue. If he tried to pee, he would shoot himself right in the eye! I could almost hear his older brother's in the background chanting, "You'll shoot your eye out!" Taunting him as all brothers do. A smile cracked across my face, and I turned away from the mirror, so I wouldn't burst out laughing. What an absurd life I was living right now...

"I'll be right back. Wash your hair," hoping the words penetrated his scripted jibber-jabber.

I paused at the top of the staircase to gain my composure before heading downstairs. Patrick and Kieran were mingling around the open doorway of the living room and met me with eager eyes at the base of the stairs.

"Did Jack super glue his penis?" Kieran asked, chomping at the bit. His eyes bright and engaged, smile smirking. My stifled laughter sputtered out unintended. Patrick began to laugh too. I waved my hands and arms, directing them into the room and closed the French door.

"Yes. He did use super glue on his body. And no, we are not going to share this with your friends!" Suddenly, my laughter ceased. I imagined how funny it was to these teenage boys. It was something you would see straight out of a scene from a movie, totally foolish and insanely funny. It was what all teen boys crave. But it is my job to instill empathy in them, empathy for Jack. Sure, we can laugh, but spreading it among their friends under the title, "stuff my brother does…" would not prove helpful.

"Seriously, this doesn't leave the house. We cannot supply any ammunition for others to make judgments about Jack," I said. Or our family, I silently thought.

"Okay, okay." Kieran said, his smirk just as wide as before.

I looked at both of them with a raised eyebrow. Patrick was trying not to laugh, his face red and pink, I turned toward the kitchen in search of oil…yellow gold. I opened the cabinet door. No vegetable oil. Crap. Olive oil should work.

I opened the glass slider and placed a folded towel to kneel on in front of the tub. Jack had a bar of soap in his hand and looked up at me.

"It won't come off." He said in a-matter-of-factly tone.

"Well this should do the trick!" I said, raising the olive oil bottle.

"Are you going to cook me?!"

"No, Jack," I said with a half laugh. "The oil will help make the glue slippery. Like soap does on your skin. This will get under the glue, making your skin slick."

"Oh," he said, looking thoughtful as he sized up my words to weigh them. His body appeared rigid as he took in the information…oil removing glue, like soap does, making it slippery…I could see the wheels turning.

"Are you sure?" he asked. "How does it work, when the soap doesn't make the glue slippery and soap is totally slippery? Like, all the time, slippery."

I smiled and grabbed a cloth and tipped the large bottle of oil into it.

"Let me see your fingers," I said, and reached for his left hand. He gave it to me, and I rubbed the cloth onto his index and thumb.

"Now, rub them together."

"Wow! I can feel my finger slide," he said, marveling at how easily they moved, he swiped them back and forth. "Okay, this works. Lay it on me, Mother!" he said loudly.

More snickers from down below. They must have opened the door.

I asked Jack to stand up and worked the oil into his skin. I started with the spot on his leg. To my relief, it did work. I gingerly peeled off a strip of dried glue. I noticed his body stiffened as I pulled the remaining section of glue off his leg, which reminded me how sensitive he was, especially with light touches or things that brushed or tickled.

"All right Jack, I am going to put the oil onto your private area to remove the glue. Just stand still for a minute," I said, as I poured more oil into the cloth.

I started to rub, peel and reapply oil all over his groin, stomach, and even his foot. It all came off, thankfully. With his skin gleaming, he popped himself back down into the tepid tub water. Subtle twirls of oil formed on top, twisting around him. He was humming and played with his action figures along the side of the tub. I leaned back against the vanity, letting out a long sigh, grateful the remainder of the evening would be filled with pajamas and bedtime stories.

My lips curled upward as I heard, "you'll shoot your eye out," chanting in my head. It was the first time in a long while I had found humor in anything related to Jack. Or found any humor in anything, for that matter. It was possible to find joy and happiness at the most absurd times. The invitation for happiness, to witness, or to embrace, was embedded into everyday moments. In feeling lighter, I could see the humor and laugh. I had moments of horror and moments of believing it was going to be okay, of dialing into myself and being present with Jack. I was not shooting for perfection, for either of us. But shooting for better—yes—better was good.

22

SUCCESS BOOK

*D*uring our next appointment with Robin, Jack's counselor, I told her about the super-glue incident. I had concerns about Jack's risky behavior, daring himself to use the glue, and afterward hiding it. He was processing the trauma of when he'd escaped from the Bradford School while transitioning into a new school environment. The behavior itself, the daring and the doing, was self-sabotage—a way to punish himself for his past. Although he'd learned about high-functioning autism, he had not yet embraced it as being a part of himself. I mean, how could he at this point? To Jack, having Asperger's was the reason he had so many problems at school. His autism ramped up his behavior, spun him out of control, and he was rejected and ostracized. Therefore, autism was bad; Jack was bad. Black and white thinking was part of the deficit. But shame, how Jack negatively viewed himself, could play a role in his behaviors as well.

It was clear we needed to take action to redirect his attention to the positive aspects of Asperger's. He needed to be built up. He needed to feel good again. Using the Asperger's picture book as a guide, Robin and Jack created their own version. Jack was the narrator and it was all about Jack's Asperger's syndrome. Many of the characteristics Danny had were the same for Jack, but a few personal additions were added, merging Jack and his diagnosis together in a real concrete way.

I collected facts and articles about well-known people who were diagnosed with ASD or shared the same characteristics with Jack. Some famous actors, like Dan Aykroyd, had come forth in recent years disclosing he had Asperger's syndrome. One night, we watched a clip from the film *Blues Brothers* of him singing and dancing. We viewed the movie, *Ghost Busters* and saw how funny he was in his role as Ray Stanz, one of the team of scientists who battled supernatural creatures with high-tech gadgets. Over the course of several days, we talked about famous men in business and historical figures who had been suspected of having ASD due to their quirky and brilliant nature. Jack liked hearing about them. He liked hearing about how smart they were and how they were often perceived as "different" by society and peers.

Jack particularly loved the story about Albert Einstein and how he forgot to put on pants one day before leaving his house. I explained that Einstein knew he needed to wear pants before he went out, but his brain was so busy thinking about other things, he forgot. Jack could identify. Jack was often reminded to flip his shirt around as it was on backward or possibly inside-out and he hadn't noticed. When he was younger, he would also put his pants on backwards too. Long after the age where typical kids figured it out, Jack was still showing up with the fly in the back.

Jack started to recognize that he was not alone. Every chance

I got, I "normalized" Jack's feelings, frustrations, individual characteristics. I pointed out similarities between these successful people and Jack. Robin offered up the idea of a "success book," for Jack. It would be part scrapbook and part therapy log, all pointing out Jack's milestones. The beginning of the book had photographs of Jack with captions of positive affirmations written below the picture. Jack reading a book at the library with the caption, "I am a great reader!" Jack hanging out with friends, "I am a good friend!" Jack giving double-thumbs-up with his Gigi in his designated bed, "I keep Gigi safe!" And many, many more. The pictures were proof of Jack's successes. The words gave a second layer of reinforcement.

In the next section of the book was Jack's ABA visuals: voice regulation chart, stoplight zones of regulation, hygiene reminders, take-a-break card with Velcro object cards and social stories. These programs had been in use for some time and Jack had even achieved many of the expected goals. It gave us another opportunity to talk about how far he had come. The next section was the therapy work that he had done with Robin. Each week they added a "success page" to Jack's book. During their session they pulled out successful threads from the past week, creating a visual list. The remarkable items ranged from earning a sticker for Gigi care, using positive language, being helpful, and getting back into the green zone. My personal favorite was, "I *successed* at everything!" Jack was getting into the groove by making positive choices each and every day. To see it compiled into one place was empowering.

Robin invited Jack and I to add success pages to reflect his growth in other outside areas, such as classes he took at our local nature center, or any badges he earned in Cub Scouts. Jack had participated in the recreation soccer program this past fall. Mike, who had coached all of the boys in soccer, coached Jack's team, making it easy for Jack and for us. Jack already knew his dad, so the transition was smooth. Jack was able to be a part of the team, spent Saturday mornings at the field with lots of families with kids of all ages, kicking the ball around having fun. We continued to follow the behavior plan, pressed him when we felt he could tolerate it, and provided positive opportunities for Jack to build his confidence. It was equally important, although I didn't recognize this at the time, for us to see him engaging in life. Trusting in ourselves to create a supportive home environment that he could springboard off from and have success was huge. We were in uncharted waters. We knew how to parent, but this was like parenting on steroids. Maybe Jack's success book was a little bit ours too.

In December, Jack finally had his appointment with a developmental pediatrician at Tufts Floating Hospital for Children. We submitted Jack's case to them, and two other specialized hospitals last May and eight months later we had an appointment. When we submitted the paperwork requesting an evaluation, we were in crisis mode. Jack had no support and no diagnosis. Now, he had an ASD diagnosis, ABA services, and he was in the beginning of transitioning back into the public-school district. We didn't expect any big revelations, just validation and further documentation by a professional in the field of child development. It would be hard to deny services for a child when they were recommended by more than one professional, especially if they were from different fields, but echoed the same treatment protocol.

Dr. Millis examined Jack, read all of Jack's history, along with interviewing Mike and me, and produced recommendations that were in line with Dr. Chamber's neuropsychological report. It felt a bit repetitive, but strategically speaking it validated the type of educational programming, setting, and supports Jack required.

Before we left her office, she paused and placed her pen down in front of her on the desktop. Looking back and forth between us, she finally spoke.

"You are Jack's biggest and best advocates. Both of you have worked so hard in giving Jack what he needs and that is not an easy road. You've done well." She smiled widely and we said our goodbyes.

I was quiet on the drive home thinking about her words, their weight resonating inside me, filling me. I thought of Mike and all we have and all we are together. I couldn't imagine doing this—any of it—without him. Maybe I don't see the scope of what I do every day, but neither does he. He never complains, just powers through. It's not what he focuses on. He focuses on us. His drive is only matched by one thing—his love for his family. I reached for his hand and gave it a squeeze as he navigated through Boston city traffic making the long ride home to Cape Cod.

23

LOOPHOLES AND LEGOS

I heard the chimes of the clock in the foyer ring, marking two o'clock. I was sitting at my computer going over the past week's emails, making a note of what needed to be discussed after the kids went to bed. I jotted down my last thought on a Post-It, then finally pulled my eyes away from the screen and peered out the window. The winter's light was fading and sunbeams reached out, catching naked branches and illuminating drifts of snow. It occurred to me it couldn't be two o'clock, more like four o'clock, the time was off again. I walked over and pulled the clock off the wall to replace the batteries and adjust the hands one more time.

It was Sunday evening, time to prep for the week ahead. Along with correspondence catch up, penciling in the weekly menu, and compiling a shopping list, there was the family calendar. I walked into the kitchen and peeled off the large calendar from the side of the fridge and called to Jack. After the third time, he pulled himself away from the game he was playing and met me at the kitchen table.

"Tomorrow you are at the school and then Lego Club is at four. I continued to rattle off the rest of the week and by the time we reached Friday's events, I noticed he seemed preoccupied.

"Are you sure I have school on Monday? Remember last time, when Mrs. Damon was sick, I couldn't go? Is she better yet?" he asked.

I had forgotten about last week, seemingly it was only a few days ago, but felt like weeks. When Mrs. Damon was out sick, we were stuck making a judgement call at the last minute on whether or not to bring him into school. His tutor would be there, but no one else to oversee him during times other than tutoring. If Jack went into a red behavior, who would help treat the behavior? Caroline and I scrambled to reach the principal to see if they were prepared for Jack but could not reach her by the time he was scheduled to be in the building. We made the decision that he would have tutoring at home instead. I worried that it may bring about a behavior, unsure of how he would accept the news, if he would believe me, or think that he was "suspended" again. It was hard to predict, but he did move through his day with tutoring at home with no incidents.

This situation highlighted a loophole in Jack's transition plan. People get sick. What were we to do if it happened again? Mrs. Paulson did return the call to Caroline later in the day and said it would have been fine if Jack came to school—that *it wasn't a big deal*...WHAT? It felt like a big deal to me! Mrs. Paulson didn't want to be the person who said he couldn't attend school due to a staff member being out sick. I am sure she didn't want the anticipated fallout of blocking a child from his education at her school, but ethically, if she didn't have staff who were properly trained (CPI and Jack's BIP), it was a problem to have him placed in a potentially unsafe environment. As far as I knew, the training had not happened yet.

This dilemma was rectified in the next version of the transition plan a few days later, noting if Jack's social worker was out, Jack would get tutored at home.

It was fair to say that I might have temporarily erased this memory. After the prior week, we'd eagerly fallen into weekend plans with friends and family. Weekends were a time to lean into other things and take a reprieve from weekday dynamics. This weekend, particularly, had been busy with an art class, cub scouting, a family birthday dinner, miscellaneous odds and ends of laundry, and fixing broken things. Jack had the Pinewood derby on Saturday. He raced a car that he and his dad had made from a kit. Jack designed and painted it. Mike helped with the construction of getting the wheels in place and the graphite to make them turn. Mike wanted Jack (and all of our boys) to take ownership of this project as much as possible. Mike, Jack, and Aidan had spent the weekend before creating their unique derby cars. Jack was excited and optimistic.

Jack and Aidan's races were scheduled close together, which was great for us because the event ran from mid-morning to mid-afternoon. It was well organized by leaders and volunteers, with chairs lined up along the sidelines, triangular flag streamers sectioning off the track, and they even supplied hot dogs and popcorn. On the left side of the racing track were three rows of chairs for parents and siblings. On the right side, against the wall, were chairs for scouts to sit and wait for their upcoming heat. Several boys from the competing dens gathered at the end of the track. They had already been directed to stay beyond the derby banners and not touch the track or the cars until the end of the race. Jack's den was large and lively. The energy in the room was electric, full of anticipation and excitement.

I sat on the spectator's side with a couple of parents I knew. I was distracted, watching the race and Jack's reactions, while trying to appear attentive to casual conversations about Elizabeth Gilbert's newest book and when spring soccer sign-ups would be. Suddenly it occurred to me: Jack was having the time of his life! He was animated, engaged, and a part of a community. He huddled with other boys, hungrily eating popcorn with bits and pieces flying, hooting and hollering as the cars raced down the tracks. In so many ways, he was just like them. An unexpected wave of warmth lapped over me. He was so complete in his happiness. In that moment, he was free to experience bliss and share it with others. I could feel my eyes begin to fill. I had slowed down long enough to see him: to see Jack, watching him be a boy and do typical things. This day was not about Jack's diagnosis or his programming. It was about joy.

"HEL-LO...MOM...MOM...EARTH TO MOM!" Jack said waving his hands at me. "I asked you about Mrs. Damon."

"Oh, sorry, Jack. Yes, as far as I know you will be in school tomorrow for Lunch Bunch, recess, and tutoring." I pointed at Monday, February 5 on the calendar. "I will pick you up at 3:20 and we will go over to set up for Lego Club at the recreation center."

"Set up? I am not doing that! You can do that," he said indignantly.

This was something I hadn't thought of. For one thing, it was a new situation with different kids, most of them he didn't know. He was unsure of what to expect. I was running the program for the recreation department, so I took a few minutes and gave him a complete picture of the routine and read the names of the kids who would be there. Unknowns were hard. When he became anxious it manifested into nail biting and verbal refusals. Jack's anxiety could make him inflexible and defensive. By talking through specifics, it should lessen his fear.

"And you know, Jack if you have any questions about the Lego club you can ask me or Faith." I reminded him. I had already told him that Faith, Jaime's mother would be helping too.

"All right, as long as you don't forget my snack!" he said, as he raced away from the table.

Standing in a sea of yoga mats, Lego bricks, and ten highly focused and slightly vibrating twelve-year-old kids felt good. Faith and I were still working out a few details about the program, but we were inspired by the creative nature of the kids. Their enthusiasm was contagious. The room we hosted the class in was huge. A former banquet hall, the building sat on the edge of a pond, with enormous glass windows facing the water, letting the light filter in, making the room feel warm even on frigid days. We brought in a massive storage bin filled with Legos. Each child had their own mat and shoe box to store their creations, safeguarding them for the following week.

As the kids were getting picked up, Faith had to leave a few minutes early to get her son off to sports practice and left me with her oldest son, and Jack and Aidan. The three of them were certainly old enough to help clean up. They organized the shoe boxes and helped me carry the monstrous bin of Legos to the car. As I was saying goodbye to the last parent and child, the boys decided to explore the building. That's when Jack went missing.

He had given me a hard time about cleaning up. His energy level had gotten increasingly higher and he was noticeably less regulated. It was five o'clock, so his ADHD medication had worn off, which was one less tool to help him stay in green. We had added this medication to curb his impulsivity and increase his focus during school hours, but we were way beyond its window of effectiveness. I directed the older boys to finish stacking the shoe boxes and to clean up any loose bricks on the wood floor and went to look for Jack.

After checking the bathroom and the office area, I was walking back toward the great room when I heard a noise that sounded like a broomstick hitting the floor. I walked further down the hall and noticed the janitor's closet ajar.

"Jack? Is that you?"

No answer. We were the last ones in the building.

"Jack?"

I slowly opened the door. There he was, in the corner of the closet, hiding behind a mop and bucket. I noticed the floor was wet as if something had spilled. My eyes scanned up and saw Jack's pants were wet too.

"Jack, I am right here...Are you okay?"

"I'm fine." His tone was tense.

"What happened?"

"Nothing."

"I see your pants and the floor is wet. Did you have an accident?" I said, keeping my voice soft. There was a pause and then he bolted right by me. He ran down the hall and into the bathroom. A door slammed with a crash. I immediately felt a wave of controlled panic wash over me. Questions flash rapidly through my mind. Would this escalate further? How was I going to get him to the car? Did I have a change of clothes to give him? Would his brother and friend notice he'd peed his pants? What should I do first, clean up the pee or go to him?

I took a breath and pulled the mop out of the bucket; with a few strokes and some cleaning spray, the floor was done. I entered the bathroom. Apparently, he'd found the women's bathroom first. There were three pink painted stalls.

"Jack, are you in there?"

No response. Bending over, I peeked under the stalls to see which one he was in, to my surprise, no feet. Maybe, I got the wrong bathroom? I heard a rustle of paper. I pushed open the middle door and it pushed back at me, smacking hard against the lock.

"Jack, it's me. It's okay. Let me see you," I said quietly.

I pushed on the door again and it swung open. He was standing on the toilet seat, his body leaning against one wall. He covered his face with his hands and let out a sob. My heart broke. The fear, the panic, and uneasiness fell away from me. All that I was left with was my child's vulnerability. I stood in the bathroom stall and placed my hand on his shoulder. I held space for him. I held space for me, too.

After a few minutes, Jack was at the sink, wiping his face and nose. It occurred to me that I had extra clothes in my car. A bag of old clothes had been rolling around the back for days now, waiting to be dropped off to the donation bin. I was sure there was a pair of pants in the mix he could wear home. While Jack changed, the other two boys and I loaded up the van. Jack agreed to get into the van only because I promised we would listen to his favorite audio book. Listening to stories was comforting for Jack. It often brought him back to himself.

I was reminded by the experience that Jack was still fragile. Today was a lot. Jack not only went to school, which included his academics (in the subset room), Lunch Bunch, and recess, but after school he'd been picked up, given a snack, and brought to Lego club. One of the kids in Lego club was in Jack's class last year at the Bradford School. Jack had been friendly with him but had not seen him much since. The combination of seeing his former classmate and entering a new environment (new rules, new kids, new room), any or all of these factors could have triggered him. Plus, his medication was slowly leaving his system. Jack had been able to hold it together until he couldn't anymore. His anxiety got the better of him, building up all day and coming to a head in the supply closet. He felt out of control, then controlled the one primal thing he could. Urination.

I was frustrated. Not at him. Not because he peed his pants. I was frustrated at myself. Even though I'd briefed him on what was going to happen and who would be there, I couldn't help but wonder if I should have intervened sooner. It replayed over and over in my mind as we drove home. It only made me realize how much pressure I was placing on myself. Of course, I wanted Jack to have continued success. But it was concerning how attached I was to his progress, as if his progress reflected on me in some way. We had become interwoven. Every fiber in my being was tuned into him. I was his personal meteorologist, observing and jotting down data, anticipating changes, and adapting when the weather became rough. But even the best meteorologist can miscalculate. All they can do is watch, analyze and prepare. It was not an exact science, and neither was Jack.

24

ACCEPTANCE

$\mathcal{A}$fter the kids were settled in for the night, I lay on my bed and closed my eyes. In recent days, there had been more communication snafus within the team. Personal dynamics were making things challenging and it had nothing to do with Jack, just egos of educators. Power struggles and positioning had brought my husband to have a private meeting with upper administration in hopes of smoothing things out. The positive thing was that Jack was doing amazing in school. He was making friends, earning opportunities for inclusion, and he was pretty happy with his progress. It was the behind the scenes drama that was wearing me down.

One evening after homework and showers had been checked off the list, I sat in the chair with a cup of my favorite tea. I pulled out my journal and began to write, releasing the chatter that had been collecting in my mind. I sat mid-stream to catch my next thought, and heard my inner voice speak.

"Acceptance is the answer to all your problems today." I was startled when I heard the voice as it was crystal clear and cutting.

"Ugh. Really? This is what you send me?" I said out loud, mildly annoyed as I was looking for a moment of peace, not unsolicited advice.

Although I was irritated by the interruption, I knew deep in my gut it was true. Several days later, I found myself in my therapist's office thinking about the message.

"I am really struggling with this idea of *acceptance is the answer*," I blurted out to her during our session.

"I can see that," Janet said and gestured to my folded arms crossing my chest.

I listed off all the reasons. Some of them were old tapes of past trespasses, things that had had been ignored and neglected. Some were current fears about timing and transition, or the dynamics of the team and the struggle to not take it personally. Monthly meetings were still ongoing, draining financial resources and precious time. I was emotionally spent returning to the same place over and over again.

We sat in the quiet, letting it fill with the sounds of the night.

"How can I accept it? How can I accept things that are unacceptable?" I asked.

After a thoughtful minute, Janet responded. "Acceptance of things we cannot change can be very freeing. Accepting a situation as it is in the moment is healing. I am not asking you to accept unacceptable behavior. I am reminding you of what you already know. We cannot change the past. Nor can you control the future. All you can do is be present in today."

"But that IS what I am doing!"

"Is it?" she asked, raising her left eyebrow. "You have done an amazing job. What you and your family have gone through, the trauma, the extinction burst, therapies, and the relentless insistence of holding a system accountable—there is no question. You have been there for him. You have put him ahead of everything else. Accepting what is right now, allows you the grace to find peace within these situations," Janet said, studying my face.

"Every time I come across a situation where they are dragging their feet, it feels personal, like they are trying to sabotage him and his accomplishments," I said, looking into my hands, feeling small.

"Part of accepting what is, is letting go...letting go of the past and the future. We accept the things we cannot change, find the courage to change what we can, and we seek the wisdom to know the difference," she said.

"The Serenity Prayer. Yes. I'm familiar. But, it's not that easy."

"It's not easy, *it's simple.*"

An uncontrollable wave of laughter filled the small room. She knew I would understand the tongue-and-cheek nature of her inference. I was not new to this concept of letting go. I had used the Serenity Prayer in the past and had found it helpful, but Jack was a child, one who could not speak for himself. Letting go felt more complicated. Although I had been running, I had become buried and weighed down by the recent fear and drama, which fed into my coping mechanism—control.

"You remember what we had discussed? You may not have control over Jack and his programming...or people, places and things, but you do have control over how you deal with it. Acceptance is a super-power."

"Yes, I have had moments, even a period of time when I

would feel peaceful and free. When I have been able to step back and trust."

"When the fear comes back, as fear does, I want you to disrupt its flow. You can recite the prayer or simply say, 'I am choosing to trust myself and the process,' and by interrupting the thoughts coming into your mind, it will break the dysfunctional cycle."

"I feel like I have gone through stages of trusting the people he is working with and trusting ourselves as his parents."

"It's been a bit of a tug-of-war, but it always is, before we fully surrender,'" she smiled.

"Where do I begin?" I asked.

"You need to get back to who you are…you said that you are a writer?"

"Ah, yes, I have always journaled…" I said, feeling perplexed by her question, as it has never been a paid vocation.

"It is at the core of who you are. Write about good things. Go back in time and find the spiritual breadcrumbs…the synchronicities that brought you here. Fill your book with pages focused on gratitude and it will transform you. You will let go…"

I allowed her words to breathe into me, filling me with hope.

25

FOLLOW HIS LEAD

"Jack wants to show you his trees," Robin, said, smiling.

Jack was sitting on the floor in a relaxed catcher's stance, swaying back and forth over two hand-drawn trees on construction paper. Printed on the bottom of the orange sheet read "Jack's Team" in big bold letters. On the red page it read "Jack's Friends" in the same spot. On each tree, bubbles with faces were attached to the branches by strings. Each individual bubble face was named.

"See, Mom, I have you and dad on the team tree with Robin and Maggie and my new teacher. I don't know her name yet, but when I do, I can write it here," he said, pointing at the space under a face with wavy hair.

"On the friends' tree, I have new and old friends. My new friends like Timmy, John, and Gabe; and old friends like Pete, Samantha and Jaime."

"Show your mom the cards." Robin gestured to the stack of index cards next to him.

"Who can I talk to about Angry Birds?" Jack said, reading the first card loudly. "I can talk to anyone about Angry Birds, but usually it's my friends," he said, answering his own question. "Next card is…Who do I talk to about my feelings?" his brow tilted inward as if he was thinking harder about this question than the previous one. "I know! Jack's team!"

"What about this one…Who do I talk to about the frustrations I had at the Bradford School?" Robin said pointing at the next card.

"Jack's team!"

"What about this one…Who do I say this to…The Webster School is the right fit?" Robin asked, giving him the card to place.

"That I say to my friends, because I am an official Webster student!" he said beaming.

"Lego Club!" he shouted, reading the next card. "My friends!"

"And what about…If I am green, yellow or red?" Robin asked with a raised brow.

"YOU!"

"Well, yes me, but who else is on Jack's team tree?"

Jack, still crouching, inched his feet closer to the orange sheet.

"There are tons of people! There's Robin, Mom, Dad, Mrs. Damon, Patrick, Kieran, Ainsley, Caroline, Maggie, Aidan and the new teacher. I would have put her name in, but I don't know it yet," he said, mentioning the mystery teacher a second time.

"Well, when you do, we can add it in," Robin assured him.

"Team trees can be added to too, no problem. And, Jack, you can take this home with you and practice with the cards. Maybe you and Mom can make up more cards." She winked in my direction. A familiar wink.

Eventually, the trees and cards would be added to his success book, along with all the other programming tools. Jack's success binder was growing thicker and thicker. I had also been working on my version of a success book, compiling good things in a journal; making gratitude lists and taking time to go out in nature was grounding. I was learning to slow down, instead of getting revved up. Downshifting into a lower gear had been both uncomfortable and blissful. I did feel more peaceful, however, so I planned to focus on believing that whatever was happening in the slowness would expand.

AFTER A "RED" behavior during a newly added OT session at school, the team decided to move the OT opportunity towards the end of Jack's transition plan. OT was quickly taken off his current schedule and his plan adjusted to reflect the change.

In spite of the recent OT setback, Jack was moving swiftly through the plan and as we approached the end of March, a year after his escape from Bradford, he was attending his new school five days a week. He was thriving and learning to navigate school during social times and during academic programming he was in the subset room with either Ainsley or Callie, Jack's new tutor from Atlas. At first, during recess, Jack stayed close to his tutor or Mrs. Damon, but over the past few weeks he had been able to interact more with peers. He even participated in flag football with a group of boys. When it got too much, he sought out his tutors. Ainsley, especially, had been his rock.

Ainsley had been with Jack since the beginning. For the past year, she'd been his consistent provider—ABA, academics, executing the behavior plan, and being his friend. Ainsley whole-heartedly believed in Jack, cheered him on, kept him in check, and gave him the structure he desperately needed. Ainsley and Jack bonded almost immediately. Maybe it was the way she read his favorite Captain Underpants series—making all of the voices and indulging in bathroom humor. Or maybe it was how she painstakingly ignored him during outbursts, holding him accountable for his behavior, but never held it against him after the dust settled. Or maybe it was because she made work fun. All of these things were true, but it ran deeper. Ainsley had won Jack's trust.

In February, anticipating Jack going to school full time, Caroline hired Callie, who could exclusively transition with Jack back into the school. Ainsley 's schedule could not accommodate the additional hours and it would be more beneficial for him to have a consistent provider for the remainder of the transition. Plus, I think we all knew Jack had become attached to Ainsley. We had talked about how Ainsley was a "calming item" for Jack. We hoped the change in tutors would help Jack gain inde-pendence.

Callie was a highly qualified Board Certified Behavior Analyst (BCBA). She cross-trained with Ainsley over several weeks before Ainsley faded out. We prepared Jack with a social story about the shift of his tutors after he got to know Callie. As if he knew, Jack had asked me after the first few days if Ainsley was leaving. I brushed him off, afraid of him having a behavior, as he had not had enough time to bond with Callie yet.

In the end, Jack had only a few yellow behaviors and one red behavior at school during the transition between staff. I anticipated it would be much worse. I think I had a more difficult time letting Ainsley go. It was hard for me to even talk about her going, because I would become emotional. I would cry anytime Caroline and I discussed the changing of staff from Ainsley to Callie. My husband would remind me that it wasn't as if someone died, and instead outlined all the good points that I could not bring myself to write in my journal. I resisted the change because my heart was aching. Instead of labeling my emotions "overly dramatic" I decided to call my friend, Mallory, since she had gone through changes with her son's paraprofessional staff.

"We had a hard time too, when Rick's provider had changed. His ABA therapist left the district," she said. "She got a new job with a private company. People come and go. It's a hard life lesson to learn, even for typical kids."

"Kids? I am having trouble as an adult! I can't stop crying about her leaving, about her not being a part of Jack's care. She not only earned Jack's trust, she has mine too."

I told her a story about a day a couple of months ago, when I was paralyzed by fear and called Ainsley twenty minutes before he was supposed to show up at school. He'd had a busy morning and was dysregulated. I told Ainsley I was afraid that Jack would have a "red" at school and maybe I should call him in sick. She talked me down by saying this, "Believe me, Nicole, Jack will hit the floor before he gets out that door (referring to Jack's past elopement)."

I believed her; she would keep him safe in spite of himself. There was no behavior that day. But, left on my own, I would have kept him home, which was the absolute wrong thing to do. She gave me the strength to let go.

"But it's not just Jack. It's me. I trust her with his life," I said quietly, tears streamed down my cheeks, making my phone wet.

"It's always hard to make these changes."

"I am not only filled with fear. I am filled with gratitude. She has become part of the family...we were so broken. She got into the trenches with us and taught us how to stand on our own."

"She was one of your first responders. You will forever hold her in a special place in your heart."

"This feels like an exercise in letting go. I have been working on acceptance and trust. It's no coincidence that I am facing this right now."

"Yeah, I find that challenging too. It's much easier to detach when it's not your own child," Mallory said. "I have been working with other families, and even though it stirred up emotions in me, I could look at their situation with a healthy level of detachment. When it's my child, it's a whole different story..."

IT WAS A BEAUTIFUL SPRING DAY, one of the first warm ones. Jack and I were at the playground. I sat on the retaining wall between the playground and the grassy area with the mature fruit trees. Jack climbed on the middle of the three trees. Over the years, all four of my children had climbed and conquered them; a rite of passage, of coming into a certain age. Jack was talking to himself happily, verbalizing a vivid scene in his head, one that came to life within the confines of the branches he scaled. I found his chatter calming. He was content and in a good place. I leaned back, reclining on my hands and tilted my face upward, as I watched him. After a few minutes, I closed my eyes, and took a breath…

"Hello down there, Mother!"

I opened my eyes to see him at the highest point of the tree —almost in the canopy. My heart dropped.

"Jack…" I said, trying not to sound alarmed. "You are a bit too high. The branches are not big enough to hold you. Climb down a little bit lower."

"Okeydokey!"

He descended from the top of the tree in a haphazard motion. He was quick and impulsive, and appeared to rely on luck. He reached the center of the tree and paused. He was standing with two feet on one branch while he held on to the limb above his head. He put one foot in front of the other, as if on a tight rope, he inched his way to the center of the branch and stopped. The limb gave a little under his weight. He noticed and began to bounce. His body had gotten lanky over the past year.

"One…two…three…" he bounced, while he held on with one hand.

I was now standing below him, wondering what he was planning, or if he was planning anything at all.

"Mom, would you be nervous if I was standing on this really strong tree limb way up high?"

"Maybe. I think I would be nervous you would fall off!"

He bounced again, making baby leaves rustle.

"But… what if there was fifteen feet of whoopee cushions below me while I was walking on it? Would you still be nervous then?"

"I'd be more nervous about the huge fart noise you were going to make if you did fall!" I said, dramatically covering my ears.

Jack let out a belly laugh that was infectious. These were aspects of him, of his true nature, that I didn't want to wish away. The awkward way he moved his body, the inner pull of curiosity that sometimes held him at bay, and his unique perspective of seeing the world.

As I watched Jack switch trees, I thought about the piles of whoopee cushions he spoke about. I imagined layers and layers of cushions protecting and supporting him. It some ways it was symbolic of Jack's Trees, scaffolding, services, supports…his programming. All of these things were put into place to help him find his balance while spotting him if he faltered. I watched Jack's body move with determination and sureness. I marveled at his capability, weaving through the limbs, focused on getting to the next level.

He was resilient. With everything, Jack had persevered. Maybe I needed to stop feeding into the fear of change—of losing Ainsley and the transition back into school—and focus on believing: believing in Jack; believing in me; believing in the divine order of things. The people who were put into our lives had made a huge difference, like Ainsley, Caroline, Jane, and Robin. I didn't see them coming and they were exactly what we needed.

There is an old saying, "when the student is ready, the teacher will appear," which I have found true in my own life. Jack was ready for the next phase. It was time for me to let go...

Several days later, Ainsley, in one of her last communication entries in Jack's log wrote about a conversation that she had with him on the school playground. He introduced himself to Ms. Stevens and Mrs. Danvers, both first grade teachers. He said that he, "feels super comfy and he is ready to join in one of their classes." Ainsley reminded him that the principal always gets to decide what kids are in which teachers' class, but that either class would be lucky to have him. He responded by saying that he was ready and would like to discuss this with the principal.

Why was I worried? Jack was clearly able to advocate for himself!

26

COMMUNICATION BREAKDOWN

*B*y the end of May, after Mike and I had repeatedly asked to be included in on any communications, emails, meetings or changes in Jack's plan, we requested copies of all correspondence between Jack's team members, from administration to public and private providers. Anyone who was sending out emails about Jack, we wanted copies. There was friction between the principal and other members of the team. The power struggle between team members had resulted in the breakdown of communication, which jeopardized Jack's programming. It was necessary to get this into order and, frankly, it was our right to be informed.

Jack was holding his own and racking up successful days, which allotted him more inclusion time in the classroom. He had adjusted to Callie and the additional hours at school beautifully. The transition plan had detailed criteria for advancement, documented and signed by Mike and I and the principal. There were no set "dates" for advancement listed on the document, leaving it open ended, as it would be impossible to foresee when he would meet the criteria to move on to the next transitional component.

What had finally prompted us to make the request for the emails was math class. Jack had met the criteria to join his class during the math block, but due to a miscommunication, Jack missed the opportunity to begin on the expected day. In addition, Mrs. Paulson wanted to write in dates for when advancement would occur, which wasn't what we agreed upon. The transition plan was systematic and rooted firmly in data. It was never meant to be executed on a whim.

When Jack was close to meeting the criteria for advancement, he would be pre-taught about the next opportunity, so he would know what to expect and when. Jack caught on to things very quickly and if there was no follow through for advancement then we were not reinforcing positive behavior. He was learning to trust his teachers and environment, and by not following the plan, it was putting Jack and the staff in a tough position. Unfortunately, this was not an isolated event. There were other times when the plan was not followed, and he was either held back or advanced without consultation with the behaviorist.

Once our request was received, communication became miraculously better. Although nothing was found in the emails, our goal was to hold them accountable. It was very likely that the superintendent would hear about this, and we had heard that in the past that the principal had been spoken to about working side-by-side with families, instead of having her own agenda. Maybe that is why things shifted.

On June 2, we finally received the end-of-the-year schedule for Jack. He would spend a total of 350 minutes in school each day (5 hours and 30 minutes). I was so thrilled for him! Not only would he be in class, but he would also participate in the traditional year-end activities, fun events such as Bubble Day, Regatta Day, Field Day, and a beach day field trip. These were social opportunities for Jack to continue to bond with peers, and with all the hard work he had put into staying regulated, he'd earned those opportunities. Coordination of supports for these upcoming events needed to be discussed. It was decided that for Jack to attend the beach field trip, his tutor and I would both be present in case he needed to be transported. For the remaining events on school property, additional staff would be added. It was up to his team to be proactive and work to ensure his safety and success.

Mrs. Paulson appeared to be more flexible and deferred to Caroline regarding specifics relating to his plan. My whole body sighed. It was a hopeful sign. I had continued to reflect on letting things go since my discussion with my therapist. My journal was filled with handwritten pages, poetry, inspirational quotes, and a feather or two. The bursting bound book was a daily ritual and gave me permission to create a space for reflection. During this time, I wrote, walked on the beach, and allowed the stillness to settle inside of me. It was uncomfortable, but necessary.

I couldn't help but reflect on the lessons of strength Mike had given to me. He was the one who initiated the demands for the emails. He was the one, at the countless team meetings, who skillfully used laser precision to get his point across to the members. He was the one, who would gather my scattered thoughts and bring me back to the most important question: *What do we want for Jack?* I had never met anyone more single-minded in getting things done. He didn't get hung up on "what ifs." He collected the information from professionals and made a plan. He didn't lament over the past. He wasn't tethered to worrying about how his message would be received but being direct and professional was a standard he held for himself and those around him. In being his partner, I learned many new skills and forged an inner strength over the past year that was continuing to evolve each day.

THE DAYS of the year zipped by and Jack completed them with ease. He even earned a school-wide award for *perseverance*. Never had one word, or one award, encompassed so much. He ended the year on a high note and transitioned into his summer schedule. For summer services, he was attending a morning day camp for the social component and tutoring with ABA services in the afternoon, four days a week. Both the camp and his sessions with Callie were located at the Bradford School, the one Jack ran from months and months ago. Jack had done beautifully being back in the building with the support of his tutor and attending camp sessions with typical peers.

It was at the Bradford School that Caroline and I met to go over Jack's progress. The mid-summer sun heated the air quickly. It was ten in the morning, but even in the shade of the oak trees I predicted we would be at the beach later to cool off. As Caroline arrived, we found a spot under the trees. With iced coffee containers in hand, we watched Jack on the field attending archery camp.

"Can you believe I got Rafferty to sign off on archery camp for Jack?" I said, laughing. "A kid who was clearing desks and

running out of buildings and single-handedly harming staff…
now armed with a bow and arrow?" I nodded in the direction of
the field where Jack stood. He took his aim at the target and
released the arrow.

"And don't forget, he took Karate camp, too!" she laughed
and raised her hands up in a celebratory way.

"Man, he has come a long way…," I said admiring him.

"Yes, he has, and that is why I believed that he could do
this." She said smiling. "You have all come a long way!
Remember where you guys were a year ago? The extinction burst,
the panic attacks, decking him on the front lawn of the water
department when he bolted from your car?"

"Yes, how could I forget?" I said sarcastically.

"You look more relaxed and at peace than I have ever seen
you, Nicole. The work you have done, the support and consistency you have given Jack, it has made a big difference. He is a
lucky boy!"

"Well, we didn't have much of a choice, did we?" I joked,
referring to the fact he was basically expelled from school.

"You had a choice." Her tone grew more serious.

"You made it possible," I said, looking at her.

She shrugged and looked back at Jack and his archery class.

"These kids, kids like Jack…they are my heart."

Tears welled in my eyes. I was full of appreciation and joy.

"Caroline…because of you, and the people who supported
him, he was able to get here. We can never thank you enough.
Thank you for saving my boy."

"My pleasure! And for the record, I can only build the plan
and create the environment that supports him to have success.
It's Jack who does the work. Just look at all he is capable of!"

We watched Jack rotate in line, wait his turn, and talk to other kids. Callie was on the sidelines, keeping an eye, but faded back enough not to impede him. His body was more animated then some of his peers and his voice slightly louder. When it was his turn, he listened to the instructor talk him through the steps. His body slowed, and he executed the instructions while he released the arrow. Jack jumped with excitement as the arrow pierced into the target and landed just shy of the center bullseye. Two other boys celebrated with Jack by giving fist bumps.

We sat and watched a few minutes more, taking in the moment, which highlighted his success. We sat in silence and absorbed his delight that radiated across the field. Then Caroline broke the silence.

"We know Jack is doing wonderfully this summer, having very little behaviors, attending camps and time spent with Callie and his other therapists have been great, but it's time to talk about transition…," Caroline's tone was ominous. "I have some news…Callie is leaving."

"What?"

"She's taking a new position in a different school district. Her last day is a week from this Friday."

I looked at Caroline.

"I know. I've already spoken to Mr. Rafferty. He wants to put one of his staff members with Jack next year, and I spoke to Jennifer about identifying a paraprofessional who is trained in autism interventions and would be able to implement his plan."

Caroline continued to expand on what this change would entail and gave examples of the proactive approach she was taking. As she made her case, my eyes focused on Jack. They were gathering up their equipment and moving on to the next activity.

I looked back at Caroline. She smiled to reassure me. She seemed confident and positive about this move.

"This is a good thing, Nicole, because I will be the one to train the new para, and the district staff, in the updated behavior plan. I am putting the finishing touches on Jack's beautiful twelve-page behavior plan. And we have already set up a time before classes begin for training."

"Twelve pages?" I asked.

"With respect to the changes in staff, they have never seen the plan before. As far as the staff who have worked with Jack, I have used more descriptors and specifics, so less opportunities for misunderstanding what the behaviors look like and how they should be treated. Last year, there were a few incidences where folks questioned, or did not treat the behaviors, and it put him at risk."

"Oh, like the incident at gym class?"

"Exactly."

During the last few weeks of school, Jack had become frustrated with another boy at the end of gym class. Jack, who was not chosen to be a helper, became upset when the other boy was not putting the equipment back correctly and called him out. The boy responded by saying, "Who are you? The cone police?" This made Jack angry and he impulsively punched the kid in the face. Embarrassed, Jack ran out of the gymnasium. Callie and other staff searched the ground floor and outside the building before Jack was found in his subset room on the second floor.

"I am not saying that everyone will do everything they are supposed to. Things happen, but it could have been avoided. With the gym class incident, Callie and I broke it down, and by replaying it, we could see she should have stepped in when Jack began cleaning up, as it was not his job in the first place."

"20/20 hindsight. Things are clearer in retrospect," I said.

"Yes, that's true. So, we adjust and tighten his plan up a bit. It's a positive thing, Nicole."

"No, I know. I am just nervous about the beginning of the new school year and this unexpected staff change...I want him to continue to be successful. To show the world what we see."

I took a deep, slow breath to ground myself. I didn't need to say yes to fear's invitation. I glanced over at the crowd of kids sitting underneath a large maple tree. Jack was among them having snack. He was chatting and eating.

"He is doing that. His behavior will go up and down. He will never be perfectly regulated, but guess what? No one is. Each day that he shows up and gets through the day, he is successful."

He was happy. And for today, that was enough.

BEFORE I KNEW IT, summer was over.

"Come on, Jack!"

I heard the sound of hands rummaging through the bookcase; books were being flipped and tossed into his school backpack, no doubt for the ride. His love for reading had blossomed since the days of reading with Ainsley on the beanbag chair. A few minutes later, Jack rounded the steps and raced into the mudroom. He had three more hard-cover books under his arm and shoved them into his bag. I handed him his lunch box. He grabbed his Keen shoes and pulled the elastic laces tight. He can tie his shoes, but it was challenging finding shoes that would last.

These Keen low hikers with the rubberized toe were hard for Jack to destroy.

Our drive to the Webster School was less than fifteen minutes. He sat in the second row, nose deep into his book, humming.

"Jack, I wanted to remind you that tomorrow you will be getting picked up for school by the school van."

"Why not a yellow bus?"

"Well, your school is too far away for the yellow bus."

"Oh, yeah. But, that's okay. I like my new school."

I felt relieved Jack was in a place of acceptance in terms of his transportation. Jack had been challenged by resisting the changes that were necessary for his growth, but over time he has seen these supports have made a difference. One reoccurring theme was that Jack's education looked different than his peers. Riding in a school van instead of a yellow bus, having a subset room (only when needed for de-escalation now), being pulled out for specific supports, and having an aide, all of these were not typical for every child, but for Jack they were necessary. His resilience was inspiring.

I fell into the lull of his humming. After a few minutes, the sound slowly faded into silence.

"But I'll miss you," he said thoughtfully, tossing his feeling into the sacred space of the minivan.

I felt the impact of his words crash into my heart. I held my breath, so I wouldn't utter the sea of emotions that filled me. If I took one sip one of air, I feared I would be overcome by this day, this precious moment and right at that moment, it wasn't about me. Because the truth was, I would miss him too.

The truth was that all of those months I had held him up

and suspended him with love, light, and sheer will, with the hope that he would rise. And he had. The truth was, once he walked out the car door, I would be left behind, a freedom I had so desperately wanted, but as it lapped upon my shore, I had feelings of trepidation. He had found his own compass. Now I needed to find mine.

"I know," I said softly. My breath was slow and measured. Internally, I counted to four, breathing in and breathing out, bringing in oxygen to calm my body, and calm my brain.

We arrived at school and I drove into the drop-off lane and took my place in line. Move and stop. Move and stop. Move and stop. Until we were next. I inhaled once more.

"Your turn Jack! Have a great day!" I said smiling, catching the last glimpse of him as he pulled open the minivan door.

Jack jumped out while he simultaneously looped his arms into the straps of his pack and ran toward the building. I watched him reach the front door and go inside with a crowd of other kids. He disappeared from sight. It was the first day he arrived on time with all the other kids. Last year, we arrived twenty-five minutes after the students, allowing the noise and commotion to die down before he entered, but not this year. His new paraprofessional, Mara, would be waiting for him in the foyer each day, and would check in with him during the walk to his second-grade class. Jack was starting his day just like everyone else.

"Fly high, Jack…," I whispered as I pulled away from the curb.

UNEXPECTED BEHAVIOR

By November, Jack had completed the transition plan, successfully adding the last two components carried over from the previous year. He was in his class most of the time, receiving individual or small group instruction as outlined in his current IEP. He was meeting new kids in his second-grade classroom and liked his teacher, Mrs. Sinclair, very much. It was reported he had two months without any elevated red zone behavior. The only slight push back had been in his reading group. Mara, his aide, had mentioned there had been some initial resistance to working with the reading specialist, but spelling had always been a challenge for him. At the November meeting, the team decided it would be helpful for him to access a motor break prior to attending the reading group to regulate his system. Due to Jack's success, they thought it was time to fade the support of his aide in specific areas of his school day.

Although Mike and I were nervous about removing support, we trusted in the decision the team proposed. Additionally, in

January, Jack would be riding the school transportation van home each day. At the time, he was getting picked up in the morning by the van, but I was collecting him at school dismissal. It was another step towards independence. The downside to him being driven home was that I wouldn't have daily access to his aide. It was reassuring to meet her at the end of the day and check in. Mara was the closest person to Jack, as Jack was her job. We had a communication sheet, but there was something about seeing her face to face. It was another opportunity for me to let go, just a little bit more. Caroline, Jack's behaviorist, was still involved with Jack's programming and I felt the team was leading us in a good direction, so we agreed to proposed changes.

As we rolled into January, Jack was moving through the fade plan, with his aide being present for approximately half of Jack's day. He had met the specific criteria on the plan, which systematically removed the aide from one area at a time. He was still getting support in most academic areas, but less during special activities, like gym and music. During lunch and recess, the monitors were told to keep an eye out for him, but not assigned to him. There was daily data to be taken on Jack's fade plan, but we soon discovered there were gaps. Although data was being taken, it lapsed during the times he was without the aide. On days when Mara was sick or they had scheduled her with a different student, Jack had an aide named Elaine. Having a second aide to rely on was a good idea. Another way to increase his independence and self-advocacy skills, but soon afterward, concerns surfaced about the accuracy in the new aide's understanding of Jack's plan.

By mid-January, Jack had expressed his dislike for a student who rode the van with him. The child on the van had a noticeable disability, which Jack pointed out, refusing to sit near him. This child would sometimes be loud, and this bothered Jack. One afternoon when he was dropped off, I asked him about the other child, and Jack stated in a factual tone that he was different than this other boy and was unclear of the reasons why he had to ride the van in the first place.

There was another child in Jack's class with visible disabilities. Her deficits were noticeable in the area of her verbal skills, as she only spoke a few words, accessing a keypad to help communicate, and she had a wheelchair with a full-time aide to help her get around. Jack had an aversion to this child as well, making subtle, but obvious physical movements to express his feelings. His social worker, Mrs. Damon, began talking about accepting other people's differences during her sessions in Jack's class. We reinforced this message at home as well.

The gaps in his programming became wider still when Caroline tightened up his home Behavior Intervention Plan (BIP) in March. We began to implement the home plan, realizing we had slid in some areas, not holding Jack to the letter in taking yellow breaks and allowing him to negotiate, or push through his task while he was in yellow. It's common, Caroline explained, for a plan needing to be adjusted and for parents (or staff) to be retrained.

As we kicked off the month of April, Jack escaped from school. This began a series of red behaviors spanning across the next two months. Although, these episodes were sporadic, they all had a reoccurring theme of rigid non-acceptance. In April, he escaped at the end of the day during dismissal. Every day the group of children who used special education transportation were dismissed first. Jack was escorted to his van before the majority of his classmates. When the rest of the student body came out into the bus loop, Jack leaped from the van. His aide had seen him and brought him back into the school lobby. Jack convinced her to let him call me, which he did, begging me to pick him up. I told him he was expected to ride the van home, which in the end, he did.

Elaine had mishandled the situation. I was grateful she caught him and then got him safely back on the van, but protocol was not followed. Not only did he call me—which is exactly what he did at the Bradford School—he showed up at home in the yellow zone. De-escalation procedures were not followed through. Mike and I soon discovered Elaine wasn't trained in the BIP by the behaviorist. An email discussion circulated in which we were trying to tease out the antecedents. Along with Jack's known aversion to students with disabilities, and the recent implementation of his home BIP, other antecedents came to light.

Although Jack's aversion to children with differences was recognized by staff, it was Jack's fear of association that provided the accelerant for his elopement. As Jack sat on the van every afternoon, he was looked on by his peers as they made their way to the buses. Too many eyeballs on Jack had always been an antecedent. The familiarity of this situation brushed against the trauma Jack had experienced at his old school, where he was labeled and shunned by his peers. The elopement from the van was right around the time of year when Jack escaped from Bradford. Cellular memories have a way of emerging around past painful events. It had been observed that Jack had been biting his nails and twirling his hair, which was a sign his anxiety had increased. Within the flurry of email communication, the term "perfectionism" was used referencing Jack holding it together at school, policing other kids when they were doing something wrong, and his aversion issues with peers.

The two behaviorists, the social worker, principal and the aide met to discuss what happened and to put in place strategies for the future. It was decided the two aides would switch off and on throughout the week to give Jack varying, but consistent support, and it would help Elaine get to know Jack better. She would also be trained by the behaviorist in Jack's plan. It was discovered that the monitoring sheets that were supposed to be filled out by Jack's activities teachers and special educators had fallen by the wayside all together, and because these forms were not being collected or even completed, there was a hole in the behavioral data. New forms would be created to simplify the process for staff. It was discussed that removing Jack's supports might have played a part in his elevated behavior. The team was in favor of the fade plan staying status quo for now, until they felt Jack was ready.

I followed up with Jennifer, trying to understand Jack's motor breaks and how they were implemented into his day. During our conversation, she told me that a "take-a-break chair" had been added to the classroom a couple of months ago for all of the students to use if they needed to reset. The teacher added a fidget box to the area, so Jack (or whoever) would have access to calming (i.e. sensory) materials. Mrs. Sinclair, Jack's teacher, was hoping to normalize having a tough moment and taking a break to regroup. Although Jack did go to the chair when directed, there was initial resistance, and he refused to use the sensory items.

As the plan at home and school synced up, providing consistent boundaries and expectations across both environments, Jack's behaviors revved. At the end of April there were four consecutive red behaviors, two of which were at home. As the calendar tipped into May, Jack escaped from me during dismissal in order to avoid a dental appointment. It was a Friday and even after giving him several reminders prior to the appointment, he still was reactive. Jack took off down the long driveway of the school. Eventually I had to drag him into the minivan. I was certain there would be calls to the office about a possible child abduction. The social worker, Mrs. Damon, saw us and parked behind me as added support. We had pulled to the side of the driveway. Cars and buses passed by as Jack swore and launched books and water bottles at my head. I ignored his behavior the best I could and prayed he would stay in the mini-van and settle down. In the end, the dentist appointment needed to be rescheduled, but he regained his composure by taking a yellow break in the car. I had not seen this heightened level of red in months. It was like we had entered a time warp back to the summer when he was in the midst of an extinction burst.

A mixture of nausea, fear and embarrassment swirled in the pit of my stomach as I drove home. Jack was in the green zone, but I directed him to read for a while as I tried to weave together the pieces of what happened. I returned a call to Mrs. Damon, who had left a message on my cell a few minutes prior. She gave me feedback about the end of Jack's day. He had gotten into the yellow zone and was a bit frustrated, using curt words with some of the kids and staff during his specialized reading group. Elaine reported he did take a motor break and when he returned, he appeared to be in the green zone, ready to work. This happened right before I picked him up, so maybe frustration lingered under the surface and when I reminded him of the dental visit, it set him off. But it felt like there was more to Jack's reactionary behavior.

In the evening, when Jack was in his pajamas and his brother, Aidan, was getting ready for bed, I took the opportunity to ask Jack about the day. We often read in our king-sized bed with lots of pillows. I read, then he read. It was our nightly routine. Also, a sneaky way for me to help him with his reading fluency.

"Jack, what happened today? Why did you run from me?"

"I didn't want to go to the dentist! I don't like the way he pokes inside my mouth!" he was getting upset thinking about it. His brow tilted and he pulled his Gigi in tighter.

"Okay, I can understand your feelings about that. How was your day before I picked you up?" I asked.

"Fine. Except reading group. The teacher smells funny and there are too many kids in the group now. I had to move to another table."

"I thought there were only three of you in the group. It's gotten bigger since the beginning of the year?"

He nodded. "Now there's like ten kids!" He said, throwing up his hands.

This may have something to do with his frustration level during the end of the day. Jack has reading four afternoons of the week and if the dynamics in the group have changed, this could be a potential catalyst.

"Who is in your group? I know your friend from Lunch Bunch is, but anyone else you know?" I asked, hoping to make a positive connection for him.

"Nope, no one I am friends with. But, Sasha's there. The one who doesn't talk from my class," he said with a sour face.

This was the girl he was having a hard time accepting. As we laid there, I stroked his hair and he leafed through the book.

"How was your spelling test today?" I asked, realizing it was Friday.

"Can I have dessert?"

"After you tell me about your test, sure."

Jack got up from the bed, collected Gigi and the book and left without another word. I was wondering how far I should push, but I knew I couldn't let him avoid the question all together. I gave myself a few minutes before I went to find him. He was in his room in bed looking at a comic book. I asked him again. Nothing.

"Jack, I need you to answer the question."

"I don't know, alright?" He exclaimed, his magazine fell to the floor and he pulled the covers over his head.

I sat and waited at the edge of his bed. I felt anxiety knock inside my chest. The push and pull of holding him accountable, knowing it could go south quickly, but sticking to the expectation, was important. I waited some more. His breath moved the sheet, making waves. Aidan came in and saw me with Jack. I gestured to him that I needed a minute. He quickly darted out of the room. Shit. I didn't want to scare Aidan off. I just needed a few more minutes with Jack. Ugh. I felt the tug of parental insecurity. *I'll check on him afterward*, I told myself, in an attempt to keep the negative self-talk at bay that was looming in the back of my mind.

"Jack, you know, no matter what—I love you. No matter what you do, what grades you get, I love you. You can tell me anything." There was a long pause.

"I failed, Okay! And I know I am going to have to stay back

—AGAIN! Or I'll have to be home-schooled by my tutor!" his voice came through clear as day through the layer of blankets and sheets.

Over the weekend, I emailed Robin about the recent red zone behavior and the conversation Jack and I had about his fears of failure. Mrs. Damon had expressed she would be doing a social autopsy on Monday morning with Jack and would reinforce to Jack that he was a Webster student. I told her that Jack had mentioned he felt he was not allowed to be sad or upset. If he was crying, he was in yellow or red. Jack was trying to hold it together all day—to be the perfect student. No wonder he felt emotional and out of control! Emails continued to circulate with Jack's team around the expression of sadness. The principal suggested dropping the colors all together. The behaviorist thought he might be seeking a loophole in the plan so that he didn't have to take a break or complete his work. Robin didn't support removing the colors as they were the grounding points in a plan he already knew. There were also concerns that if we removed the language, we would fall away from treating his behavior as a child with autism.

A few days later, Jack had another episode at dismissal. The van was held, and he was brought to the subset room to deescalate. He was placed on the bus with Mrs. Damon, the aide and the principal. It was a rocky ride home for all involved. Although he appeared to be in green getting back on the bus, he was placed on the bus with an entourage of staff, which was a trigger. After the episode, the behaviorist recommended a harness be shown to him as a deterrent for future behavior. She also wrote a new social story, not only outlining expected and unexpected behavior, but also adding a reward system to his programming. If

Jack had "expected behavior" in school (doing his work, no red zone, taking a break, etc.) he earned electronics time at home. If he had unexpected behaviors, then he didn't earn time. Video games were a preferred activity and the behaviorist was looking to capitalize on this to help curb his recent red zone behaviors.

The new social story and reinforcement earning system went into place in the second week of June. As we waited word of Jack's schedule for his summer programing, we learned his principal gave her resignation, and was leaving at the end of the school year. Although, I wasn't sad to see her go, the thought of a new principal made me a bit uneasy. With two weeks left in the school year, we finally heard that Jack's summer sessions wouldn't be in a group setting but working one-to-one with a special educator in the areas of math and reading. There was no camp or social component offered this year, so Mike and I opted to pay for sailing lessons with the recreation department. He would continue to have OT over the summer to work on fine motor skills and tools for regulation and sensory processing. With the new reinforcement plan in place and the knowledge of Jack's future, his remaining school days in June were successful.

28

SAILING LESSONS

*E*nding the year on good footing was a relief, but there was little rest and celebration. The time between the last day of school and the beginning of the summer session was just under three weeks. With our other kids, it was easy to plunge into the lull of summer vacation, letting the tides be our guide and allowing schedules to fall by the wayside. With Jack, I wasn't able to be so relaxed. In the near future I was looking at two separate transitions. One was summer programming (lasting six weeks) and the other was going into a new school year. Luckily, his second-grade teacher would be looping with Jack and his class. That was Mae Paulson's parting gift to Jack. He would have the same teacher and the same kids next year. It was reassuring that he would have a familiar teacher, kids and support system in place. The big changes in September would be working with a different reading teacher and the school's brand-new principal.

For Mike and me, having a new principal at the Webster School was an unknown. Like Mae Paulson, he had the final say in what went on within the school and how things were done. With Mrs. Paulson, she wasn't willing to let other professionals take the lead in "her building," thus creating tension among team members. It created a divide and communication errors; Jack's programming, suffered from it. Our hope was that Mr. Wall, the new principal, would want to work with all of the members of Jack's existing team and value what they brought to the table.

I knew if I didn't keep a schedule in between summer school and the regular school year, it would backfire. Jack needed structure in his day, a blend of non-preferred tasks with summer fun activities seemed like the best way to go. We had our home behavior plan in place and kept the language of unexpected and expected flowing. Consistency was key. We stayed on track with bedtime routines and getting up in the morning.

It wasn't until we were halfway through the summer I decided to check in with my own therapist as it had been a couple of months since our last session. I had been taking walks when Jack was with his tutor, along with an occasional yoga class, but my energy had been dispersed elsewhere. Patrick was working as a lifeguard and Aidan had various activities and play dates. Kieran was participating in a volunteer program at his high school sprucing up the outdoor fitness trails. Everyone had someplace to be and, most of the time, I was the driver. A few times, I double booked myself. Apparently, I believed I could teleport myself at light speed across town in a flash. Laws of physics didn't apply when I penciled it in on our family calendar. This left little time to think about me, so when I landed in the familiar chair in my therapist's office, it took me a while to settle in.

"Are you breathing?" she asked with a raised eyebrow.

"Somewhat." I said, avoiding the depths of her question.

"So, Jack's doing well with his summer sessions and it sounds like he has been regulated since the end of school?"

"Yes, he has, but I feel like I am on pins and needles, waiting for him to react. The end of the year ignited anxiety within me."

"It triggered the past, much of which you're still recovering from. Survival mode was a real thing for you in his first year back. Not only did Jack experience trauma, you did as well. I see your anger has lifted a bit, maybe we can begin to work on your fear."

I didn't want to hear that I had work to do. Seriously? My life was work. Structure and planning and consistent boundaries... blah, blah, blah. Everything I did had meaning and purpose. Why couldn't I sit there and complain a little while longer? Lament over the fact his old principal bribed him with candy to ride on the transport van, totally disregarding his behavior plan? Or complain that I was late—again—for picking Patrick up at work? Or highlight the fact that I still didn't know who Jack's aide would be in September?

She just sat there and waited. Ugh, she was waiting *me* out.

It was familiar to fall into the role of the human doer, the mom, the executer of all things necessary. It was easy for me to become a victim, because in many ways I felt like I was. I had been carrying the residue of anger and fear around with me, and as I sat stationary, I felt sadness tug at me like a forgotten child.

"I want you to acknowledge not just Jack's success, but yours too. Take a minute and close your eyes. Visualize yourself standing tall, speaking up for Jack at the meetings, being the communication hub for his providers, juggling the responsibilities of home and caring for your children. See yourself as you are…strong, wise, and loving," she said in a calm silky tone. "You can trust in your ability to be there for your children. You can trust that you have surrounded yourself with people who are supportive. You have cultivated an environment that's healthy and sustaining for your family. In your mind, name your fears. Take a deep breath. Now, breathe out the fears and let them go," she said.

My mind swirled around the fears. My breath was like smoke, dancing and encircling each one. There it was: fear of Jack getting hurt or hurting someone else; fear of what others thought about him and how their assessments impacted him; fear about living through another extinction burst like last summer; fear of not being the right mother for Jack, not able to give him what he needed to progress. With tears streaming down my cheeks I pushed air from my lungs. I imagined the smoke pouring out. It pulled each strand of fear, dispersing each one into the air. I saw them float under the windowpane, their energy and power transmuted as they drifted into the salt marsh. I thought of the areas I had changed. I wasn't the same woman a year ago. I was more confident than I had ever been before.

"I know that fear has been a block for me," I said.

"But it doesn't have to be. In our sessions, we have acknowledged the past, and the fears keeping you bonded, so now you can move on," she said with a smile.

We agreed I would recite a daily mantra about trust and keep journaling about releasing fear. I recognized I had shut down last spring in response to Jack's elevated behavior. It was simply self-preservation. There was no room for me to feel. But I had done what was needed for Jack, and it was time to take care of myself.

ANOTHER WEEK HAD PASSED. Jack had been at sailing lessons for two weeks and had been equally excited and exasperated learning how to sail and navigate around the lake. To my surprise, he enjoyed "Capsize Day," but later in the week I heard him shouting orders at his sailing partner as they drifted away from the group. The instructors had seen Jack's boat and circled back in their little powered dingy to assist them. In the end he took instruction and the boat was righted. But there was no aide or place to take a yellow break on tiny sailboat. It was a real-life situation and I was pleased he came back to his center.

Regardless, I was definitely out of my comfort zone. I planted myself in the beach area next to the boathouse. I journaled and continued my push-pull relationship with fear and trust while I waited during the two-hour class. To mark the end of the session, the instructors put on "Pirate Day." It was a treasure-seeking competition using boats to sail to the small islands within the lake to gather clues to where the pirate's booty was buried. Teams of two worked together on this epic journey, using the skills and knowledge they had accumulated over the past few weeks.

Raising the bar even higher, Jack's eldest brothers had talked about pirate day for years. Kieran's pirating stories were legendary. Jack had even heard the instructors talk about Kieran's feats to get the gold, probably as a cautionary tale, but I got the feeling there was a thread of "can you believe that kid?" mixed with equal admiration of the stories they told. Competition ran deep, as both Patrick and Kieran were in the same class. Mayhem ensued; there was sabotage, boat tipping and mast scaling.

Thankfully no one got hurt, and although it was never directly said, new rules were put into place after the year of the Donovan boys.

The majority of the competition took place on the water and on the sister islands in the center of the lake. I watched as they sailed offshore. The sailing instructors traveled behind in their motorboat. Jack's boat had a rainbow sail with a fish on it. He was at the stern and his partner in the middle of the boat as they gently moved to the first island. I felt relieved that I could see which boat he was on, but as they glided away I began to feel uncomfortable. Fear was bubbling up. As the boats diminished in size, I started to laugh. By myself, in my beach chair at the edge of the pond, I burst out in uncontrollable belly laughter.

It struck me hard. I had absolutely *no control*. No control over Jack and his behaviors or emotions. He was on a freaking boat in the middle of the lake! If shit was going down, I had no way of intervening or protecting him. And at the heart of it all, control had been riding shotgun in my life. I had been determined to keep things afloat and flowing smoothly. No bumps. No detours allowed. As I sat, feeling uncomfortable, it was crystal clear to me. It wasn't about Jack on the lake. *It was every-thing*...and control was an illusion. Even with the matrix of support, it was up to him. In addition, he was a human child. He would have missteps. Why were my expectations for him greater than any of his brothers? Was it because the stakes were high? That our options were limited? We were pioneering a trial, cobbling together a program in the public-school system with hopes it would work. I couldn't control it all. I planted the seeds, fertilized, watered and nurtured the garden, but in the end other influences would play a part. Factors like the sun, the environment and Jack.

Time crawled as I watched the boats crisscross from island to island. I could barely make out the differences in the sails, but I did see a couple of bodies jumping ship before making land. The sound of laughter and yelling echoed across the calm water. I took another breath and closed my eyes and listened to the sound of competition, discovery and excitement. These were the sounds of childhood and no matter what happened on the water, it was another opportunity for Jack to grow. Hell, it was also an opportunity for me to grow, too. Why did I let my fear override my excitement of his independence?

I took another breath and slowly release the air from my lungs. A moment later, I felt something tickle my foot. I glanced down to see that a dragonfly had landed on the top of my foot. Its wings shimmered in the sunlight and the deep blue of its body had an iridescent glow. Earlier in the week a friend shared with me her encounter with a bunch of dragonflies while visiting her sister's grave. It was as if they were performing a dance of celebration for her. She looked up the spiritual meaning for the dragonfly when she got home and when she told me what she found, I got goosebumps. The symbolism of the dragonfly is one of transformation and adaptability. To see beyond the illusion of what is on the surface and to find the joy in the moment. For my dear friend, the spirit of the dragonfly invited her to feel happiness for her sister's transformation. It was a powerful message, one my friend needed to hear.

As I watched the dragonfly dart off and skim along the top of the water, I heard my inner voice say, "thank you." I acknowledged nature's nod to me, the synchronicities of hearing about my friend's experience just days prior and being touched by the dragonfly at that exact moment and felt a wave of peace wash over me. Fear is the illusion. I can't control Jack, or anyone else for that matter. Transformation was happening before my very eyes, in Jack and in me. We were loved and supported. And no matter how things played out, we would be okay.

Sounds of victory bellowed out from the path that led to the boathouse. The pirates landed back on shore. I began to pack up, tucked my folded chair under my arm and headed for the boathouse. I arrived at the clearing and saw the group of outlaws eating their bounty of snacks. Jack was talking with another child who was holding a golden trophy. Jack saw me and broke his conversation mid-stream to announce his buddy, Sam, was victorious.

"Sam won! Sam is just like Captain Kid, mom!" he said loudly. Sam's smile widened. And so did Jack's.

"My boat came in third, but not last!" he said in a quieter tone, as he pointed over to two boys sitting together chewing on Twizzlers. "But it doesn't matter, because we all share in the captain's treasure!" he said as he shoved a small white cupcake into his mouth.

Victory is best when shared, I thought as I watched Jack celebrate with his peers. Transformation and adaptability were ever present. My heart softened as the day's awareness took hold. Letting go of fear, of the illusion of control, was freeing. To witness Jack's success as he navigated new situations was icing on the cupcake.

WE WERE FILLING in the final days of summer vacation. Our annual trip to Flume Town, USA, was underway. Underneath the cabana, Faith and I kept home base secure, while other moms and kids explored the water park. The boys were paired up with friends and our cabana was centrally located. I had been more at ease since my revelation during sailing lessons.

"I've decided to go back to work, part-time," the words blurted out in a stream as Faith and I were catching up.

"What? That's awesome Nicole!"

"I am returning to the preschool program I had left when Jack was home schooled. They were looking for a teacher and I took the position. I feel like I need something for myself. And I did leave so abruptly two years ago," I said feeling my eyes drift away from hers.

"Well, you had to leave. And they respected your choice. You don't have to go and prove anything to anyone or make up for lost time. They are lucky to have you!"

The truth was, I did feel I had something to prove. At the time, I didn't want to admit it. I had guilt from leaving my teaching position, which intellectually I knew it was ridiculous, but there was something inside of me that needed to go back. Maybe I needed a return to normalcy. For sure, our bank account would thank me. It was not only the loss of income, but the added expenses of copays and paying out-of-pocket for other services not covered by our insurance, as well. It was also an opportunity to take some of the focus off of Jack, to find balance and regain my sense of purpose. It was an exercise in letting go and giving space for everyone to breathe, to do their jobs. Of course, I would still be involved and connecting with his support staff and teachers. I would always be his "person," but I needed something else.

"I am Captain Underpants!" a loud voice broke through my stream of thought as a streak of red ran by us.

"Come back, Jack!" I heard his brother, Kieran yell.

Patrick and Kieran piled under the shade of our rented cabana and began to ransack the cooler. Hungry hands and mouths feasted, as Jack continued to run back and forth on the grassy strip in front of the cabana tents. He had on a red and blue bathing suit and red towel which he held at his neck. The beach towel kicked up behind him creating a wave. He was flying, or at least he thought he was. Apparently, food had been a good distraction, as Patrick and Kieran had forgotten about dragging Jack to the highest flume, a new one that year.

"I escaped captivity! That was a close one!" Jack said as he plopped himself down on the blanket after watching his older brothers leave.

OVER THE NEXT FEW WEEKS, we prepared to go back to school. Jack met the new principal during the annual "see the classrooms" night at school. Mr. Wall was stationed in the library for a "meet and greet" opportunity. Jack stood in line for a long time and although I could sense he was nervous, he shook Mr. Wall's hand and introduced himself. There was no eye-contact from Jack, but this wasn't unusual. During the short exchange of small talk, I wondered if Mr. Wall knew who Jack was. We scaled the steps to the second floor to see Jack's third grade classroom. Desks were arranged in groupings of four or five. Mrs. Sinclair had taped name tags to the assigned desks. Jack weaved through the groups of desks to find his seat. His friend Will was in his group. A look of satisfaction spread over his face. He poked around in the book area and took in the various charts and schedules on the board.

As August was coming to an end, I too was spending time in the classroom. At the Montessori Children's House, I was cleaning and setting up materials for the new school year. Trays were prepared with practical life works, shelves were wiped and rearranged with books about harvesting, nature, and social skills. It was a new year, with new possibilities. I was hopeful and excited. I was returning to a job I loved with a new perspective. I had more tools in my toolbox to bring to the classroom, a deeper level of understanding and a bigger heart.

29

TRANSITIONS

*W*e were midway through October when I realized I had made a mistake. I was not ready to be back in the classroom and be teaching again. On heavy days, there were seventeen students and two teachers: me and my assistant. The classroom consisted of mostly active boys. And, let's face it, it was an energy I was very familiar with, but in a classroom setting I needed to create a calm learning atmosphere. I brought movement and motor breaks into our daily routine to help keep them focused and engaged. Being a Montessori class-room, the children are mostly self-guided. Materials are organized and put into baskets or on trays, which the child can take out themselves to explore. Lessons by the teacher are given either one-to-one or in small groups. The philosophy of Montessori is to "follow the child," as they will lead us to whatever they are drawn to learn. In a mixed-aged-classroom of preschool children ages three through six, ground rules and routines were necessary for a classroom to feel safe and be productive.

I was well versed in Montessori and believed in their philosophy and teachings. I created the environment with intention and care. It was inviting, bright and clean. I had anticipated there would be an adjustment period, for both my students and me. Some things came together nicely, but others didn't. By the beginning of November, I had identified a handful of students that exhibited non-typical behaviors. They ranged from subtle sensitivities to sound, light and movement to blatant presentations of aggression, running away, lack of engagement, and stimming. It made me question, *am I really seeing what I am seeing?* Or was I transposing my own experience into this new one?

I spent hours talking to staff, child development professionals and reading articles on classroom management. At one point, we called a meeting with one of the children's parents and presented our observations of the child. We suggested they consult their pediatrician, as our team felt their child would benefit from further evaluations and testing. It was not an easy conversation, and the parents were having a hard time digesting the information. In the forefront of my mind, I kept thinking about my own experiences with my son and how I wished someone was as up front and candid with me when he was in preschool. I wanted to tell them how lucky they were to have an opportunity to explore and be aware of their child's differences. But, "different" to them was a bad word. To be different was one of their biggest fears. I read their body language and felt the wall of disbelief being built as our conversation veered down this path.

The child was pulled from our program a few weeks later. I heard they were seeking an evaluation, but interactions with the family in their remaining time with us were strained. It hurt my heart that the news was not taken well. Did they know I loved their child? I came to bat for this kid, knowing we would probably lose him, and being a small private school, every dime was counted and utilized. I knew in my gut it was the right thing to do. I spoke for the child, and although I couldn't control how it was received, to not say anything would have been a disservice for all involved.

Meanwhile, Jack was having a great transition into the new school year. In November, the data revealed he only had four yellow zone behaviors and no red. The fade plan resumed, and new monitoring sheets were implemented to collect data on his behavior. As discussed, they had been reworked and simplified for staff. It was going so smoothly, Mr. Rafferty proposed the removal of the outside BCBA, Caroline Chase. We agreed to keep her on as a consultant, though Mr. Rafferty made it clear that we would be required to go through Jennifer Booth, the district's BCBA, as the contact for his IEP and behavior plan. We reluctantly agreed. Again, we had no grounds to say no. The data reflected how well Jack was doing, but we had concerns about how much time she would have to monitor his programming. I knew Jack required a keen eye, but it also gave me the opportunity to step back and see how he did.

As we rolled through December there was an incident before Christmas break. It was reported, but not witnessed, that Jack had squished another student's sandwich during lunch. The child "gave Jack the middle finger," and Jack responded by pressing his hand down on the child's peanut butter and jelly. The details were a bit unclear, and it was handled as a yellow zone behavior, not as a red. In January, as we were settling back from holiday vacation, Jack slapped his friend Gabe across the face during library. Jack's aide was present but stood away from Jack. She observed Jack becoming frustrated with Gabe during check-out time. Gabe was the library helper, scanning the books out for each child. The line was slow moving and Jack began to direct Gabe in how to "move it along better," and appeared frustrated when Gabe ignored him. Before the aide could step in, Jack reached over and slapped him. As he explained to the aide after his removal and break in the subset room, he was angry at Gabe because his slowness jeopardized Jack's reading time.

The behavior was uncalled for and unacceptable, for sure. In a slew of emails following this event, Mr. Wall determined Jack would be disciplined as outlined in the school's code of conduct. Mike and I fully agreed his actions deserved and required consequences but felt it should be noted his behavior stemmed from his autism disability and it should be addressed through his behavior plan under the direction of the behaviorist; but, it wasn't. Jack received an in-house suspension and was required to do his work with his aide in the office conference room for the day.

Our concerns for recognizing and identifying Jack's antecedents for his reaction to Gabe (and the sandwich incident) went beyond a suspension. His behavior came from anxiety, rigid thinking and a lack of perspective-taking. All of these had been documented as being a part of his disabilities. Mrs. Damon did conduct a social autopsy with Jack to discuss different strategies he could have used. Mike and I feared that the focus was on his reaction, rather than the root cause. We were also told that Jack had been avoiding "yellow protocol" by way of using the bathroom. Jennifer Booth was to address this new behavior in an updated BIP.

To add to Jack's anxiety, in January we had several snowstorms, one of which was a blizzard where we lost power and our street remained unplowed for three days. Jack had extreme fear of the dark, specifically when the power went out. Bloodcurdling screams in the middle of the night always followed a power outage. This series of school closures after Christmas vacation and his suspension didn't give him a chance to get into the groove. On a snowy afternoon in early February, as the kids were packing up at the end of the day, Jack took a paperclip and put it inside an electrical socket. It was at this point that Caroline was called back in to consult.

In a phone conversation, Caroline described her observations while she was in Jack's classroom. She saw a difference between how Jack was treated versus his peers. If another boy said a sassy remark, the teacher might give a sign, or a look, and the child was redirected. If Jack made the same remark, he was either given a warning or sent to the take-a-break chair. He had become aware that the expectations for him were higher than his peers. She further noted that we had a clinician in charge of his BIP. Even though Jennifer was a BCBA, her approach was from a broader psychological perspective, not of the precise nature of behaviorism. There was more room for interpretation. With Jennifer, the data wasn't the driving influence in how she determined where Jack's behaviors stemmed from. Relying on the occasional visit, but mostly secondhand observations of Jack, her perceptions were more subjective. This made it difficult to track, specifically the subtle ways Jack shifted his behavior. In the past, when Caroline was the lead on Jack's case, she gathered information by direct observation of Jack and the statistics formulated from the data. Caroline highlighted the fact we were dealing with two different behavioral approaches.

The district invited both of the behaviorists and the social worker to consult upon the paperclip incident. The whole team met a week later to go over their findings. The divide became more evident when we gathered to discuss Jack. Jennifer passed out a reformatted version of the BIP, one Caroline had not seen yet. Caroline had been the creator of Jack's BIPs in the past and when they had been executed properly, were hugely successful. Caroline said she was surprised by this new version, as she was under the impression that they would be working on it together. Jennifer responded by saying she could get her input today and add it into the working document.

"We are seeing a different Jack this year," Mrs. Damon responded as the paperclip incident surfaced.

"What do you mean?" I asked.

"His actions seem more deliberate, like they are planned." Mrs. Damon responded.

"What you're seeing is *old behavior*. This is how he presented at home during the extinction burst," Caroline stated.

"Even with conducting the social autopsy after each event recently, I feel like I am getting the feedback I want to hear, but there is a lack of understanding of how his actions are affecting others," Mrs. Damon said.

"But, isn't that part of his autism? Jack struggles with taking other people's perspectives. It's part of his disability," Caroline responded.

"Most kids with autism struggle in the area of empathy, but they can develop skills to expand their understanding," Jane said.

"Going through the social autopsy is great, but the key component is helping him understand how it impacts and affects others. We need to help him connect ALL of the pieces," Caroline explained.

"I hate to report this, but Jack's behaviors are starting to have an impact on him socially. He is not getting picked during activities and kids are hesitant to sit next to him at lunch," Mrs. Sinclair added.

The conversation turned back to safety. Jennifer brought up an incident that had occurred at home last year. Jack had lit a few matches. We had discussed it during one of the meetings and Robin noted they created a book about safety as a strategy. Jack and I had worked on the book, adding rules ranging from fire, to public and household safety. The tone shifted from safety to Jack having a possible "fascination" with fire. This was concerning because, once again, we were going down a clinical path. I became frustrated that the school behaviorist and social worker were linking these two events and hinting that it could stem from mental illness. We'd had extensive neurological tests completed, countless evaluations, and he worked weekly with Robin, his therapist, and all of them identified Jack's autism as being the primary deficit.

"Tell me, how many eyes were on him when he put the paperclip into the electrical socket? Caroline asked Mrs. Sinclair.

"Well, the whole class. We were all getting ready to go home when it happened," she responded.

"Attention seeking is one of the functions of Jack's behavior. Time and time again we have seen this. Everyone in his class saw him. When he was removed, were they all watching him as well?" Caroline questioned.

"Yes. Mrs. Damon arrived a few minutes later he was escorted to the subset room."

"We need to flush out what the true antecedents are here. Jack has a neurological difference and his behaviors manifest out of his autism disability," Caroline added strongly, appearing a bit frustrated. "We know Jack's beginning to feel the impact of his actions from his peers. He has had resistance to accessing yellow breaks, aversions to special needs kids and being associated with them, and he polices kids to follow by the rules. The rigidness, his drive to be perfect, can be seen as an antecedent to his maladaptive behaviors," Caroline pointed out.

As the conversation continued, it was revealed that some of the data had not been consistently collected, or graphed. The team assigned one person to collect the data to help streamline the process. In the revised BIP, Jennifer removed "yellow bag" from the document, leaving the team to discuss implementation of movement strategies to use as de-escalation tools to replace the yellow bag (which had not been used in months). Laminated picture cards were to be created depicting the movement activities Jack could do when he was escalated. They were to be posted inside the subset room and his aide would also have a copy on his clipboard that she carried at all times.

The team revisited Jack's aversion to the color scheme of his zones of regulation and discussed shifting the language to be more palatable for him. Mrs. Damon brought up an analogy of a soda bottle. When it was sitting untouched, the soda was flat and "in the bottle." When it was disrupted, it became "bubbly." If it was tossed it became "fizzy," and when it got shaken up, it "blew the top off," explosive and unexpected. These were great visuals for Jack. The team would align the soda bottle language with the colors of the zones, at least in the beginning, allowing him to make the connection. It would be a five-point scale, adding in blue and orange, giving him a bigger range of emotions to tap into. The same protocol would apply; he would utilize the take-a-break chair, the subset room and motor breaks as outlined. The behaviorists, Mrs. Damon, Robin and Mr. Wall would be collaborating on creating the "soda bottle behavior plan," and scheduled a time to meet the following week.

30

REFLECTIONS

I snuck into the end of the play rehearsal hoping to get a glimpse of Aidan. He had been part of the stage crew, working behind the scenes, and recently one of the directors had asked him to take a small role. He would be moving around with the other cast members, so it was less intimidating for him, but still, for him to stand in front of a crowd, even in a group was a risk. Aidan had become guarded since Jack left the Bradford School. He had a couple good friends, but was not part of a social crowd, nor had he been interested in school activities. When his best friend encouraged him to join the theatre crew, I was pleasantly surprised Aidan signed on. As I watched him on stage during the rehearsals navigating the choreographed scene and hitting marks with the cast, my heart filled with joy. He was finding his way and learning to trust his world and himself a little more.

So much of my focus had been on Jack that I often struggled with feeling guilty that my attention was unevenly distributed, but in my core, I knew I was dancing as fast as I could. Patrick had his first home soccer game, which I would run off to, hoping to catch the last half after play rehearsal. I looked over at Jack sitting next to me. He wasn't watching his brother. Instead he was reading his favorite comic book, *The Adventures of Tin-Tin*. His feet swung back and forth, bringing a soft vibration to the seats around him. He was kinetic and in motion, just like his mother.

"And that's a wrap, folks!" the director announced after the scene ended.

Kids scurried to gather backpacks and jackets, their voices were loud and electric. Aidan appeared out from the curtain with a smile. Oh good, he looked happy. I hoped he wouldn't give me grief when I mentioned we would be swinging by Patrick's game. He gave me an eye-roll, but considering he was on the threshold of becoming an official teenager, I deemed it age appropriate. It made me think about how I would handle an eye-roll from Jack...would that response be a yellow?

The soccer game was at the high school. I searched the fields for blue and gold uniforms until I found his team around the back of the building. Although we could view the game from the car, I walked out to the sidelines where a few other brave parents stood. The calendar said April, but the weather was cold and moody. Maybe spring would arrive soon. It was more of a plea than a prayer. After the winter we'd had, with numerous storms and inches upon inches of snow, I was done with these raw gloomy days.

I caught Patrick's eye and he gave me a nod. Mike had been Patrick's soccer coach forever, which meant two things. First, I didn't have to learn the rules because Mike had that covered. And second, because Mike was Patrick's coach and dad, I skipped out on a lot of games. Even though Mike was coaching that afternoon, I showed up. It was important not to just watch Patrick play, but to *see him*.

"Mom, why were you standing with the opposing team's parents?" Patrick asked me at the dinner table that evening.

"What?" I said, through a mouthful of salad.

"You were on the *wrong side*," he said.

"Oh Mom! You did it AGAIN…?" Kieran remarked, through laughter.

"Yeah, I tried to wave you over during the game, but you didn't seem to notice," Mike chimed in.

All of the boys were laughing and poking fun at me. This is one of my best roles. For whatever reason, my boys think I am funny. As I looked around at their smiling faces, it didn't bother me to be the butt of the joke. I knew why I was there, and it didn't bother me in the least to shout for Patrick and his team among a group of rivals. And, more importantly, Patrick knew why I was there, and that was what mattered.

I ACCIDENTALLY BOOKED my mother and me on a first-class flight from Boston to Turks and Caicos. In the chaos of getting ready for a long-awaited girl's vacation, I had no idea until we showed up at the airport. I took it as a sign that we both deserved a bit of luxury and extra care. The trip was to celebrate my college graduation. I had completed my undergraduate degree, twenty-plus years in the making, and my mom gifted me a dream vacation. I had put the trip off as I'd completed my last college course right around the time Jack's behavior spiked. We celebrated my big graduation day at a local restaurant, inviting family and close friends, which was very special, but the vacation went on the back burner.

Now, here we were, off to a beautiful island for a whole week. No kids. No work. No responsibilities. I looked forward to spending time with my mother and lazy days on the beach. Although it would be a vacation, I mentally scheduled time for personal reflection. The ripples of Jack's energy and his recent acting out at school had been challenging, and the stress at work didn't make it easier. My work life and home life had become mirrored. The squeeze at my job was both real and self-imposed. I was managing classroom behaviors while trying not make it worse. I didn't want to reinforce problematic behaviors, but I was struggling. The reality was, I taught at a private school with limited resources and staff. There was no behaviorist or social worker to be called in when a child was clearing shelves. If the parents were not on board or were inconsistent in supporting the expectations at home, it made it harder for us during the school day.

I remembered how angry I felt when Jack's educators were reinforcing his behaviors…the phone calls home, the attention, and the removal from the classroom that allowed him to escape from completing his work. And here I was, feeling like I was becoming more of the problem, rather than part of the solution.

It took me several days to unwind. The weather was tropical, the sun was shining, and the beach was postcard perfect. One afternoon, as I was floating in the ocean, it came to me. From some place deep inside, I knew I had to leave my current teaching position. This revelation was scary. Professionally, it was all I had ever known. What was I even qualified to do? Fear began to creep in…I brought my awareness back to floating. Back to my breath. Back to the ease of being on vacation, adrift in Grace Bay. I laughed out loud as the name couldn't have been more relevant. I felt the gentle waves wrinkle my fingertips as I began to let go…

After April vacation, Jack's team put his new BIP in place. A conference call with Jennifer Booth, Mr. Wall, and Mrs. Damon was conducted to help me understand the new "soda bottle" language. I asked specific questions about how to implement this same BIP at home, but I didn't feel confident in the answers they gave. The new BIP was clearly school based. We would need our home plan to be consistent with the school plan, otherwise it would not only be confusing, it could present loopholes that Jack would find. With the implementation of the adapted plan, along with the last few months of bumpy behaviors, I was aware we could be headed for an extinction burst.

I received a call in the middle of May alerting me of a spike in Jack's behavior. As I arrived at the school, I saw two police cruisers parked outside. As I entered the building another mom made a comment about the police cars. A weak smile curled my lips in response, as I knew they were here for Jack. As I approached the main desk, I was quickly brought into Mr. Wall's office. One police officer was there, along with the principal. Mr. Wall explained he had just come in from a meeting off campus and was gathering information about what had happened. Apparently, the school's assistant principal had phoned the police after Jack had gone into the subset room. He was thrashing around and kicking at walls. At one point, he scaled up to the ceiling, popped the ceiling tiles free and pulled out the phone wires, which disconnected service to the office next door. I asked to see him, but the officer said I needed to wait. He was in the process of finally calming down in the subset room.

The officer began to question me. Most of the questions pointed toward Jack's mental stability. We were four questions in when I repeated my request to see my son. It was clear where he was going with his line of inquiry when he suggested they could call an ambulance to bring him to a local hospital for a formal evaluation. It felt like I had been punched in the gut. He didn't get it. I reiterated that Jack had had several evaluations and that his diagnosis was autism. I was angry. And I was scared.

When we got to the subset room, I was greeted by an entourage of people standing outside the doorway in the common room. There were three rooms off of this common area. Jack's subset room was the middle room, sandwiched by a conference room and a small office. In attendance were Jack's social worker, the assistant principal, Jennifer Booth, Mr. Wall, both police officers, Jack's aide and the janitor. Yes, the janitor. Was he part of the muscles for transport or clean up? I am still unsure. Regardless...*so many eyeballs*. Jack saw me through the window of the door. He pleaded with me through the glass. I ignored him, as the plan had instructed. Five long minutes later, he had gotten back into green. He came out of the room. I directed him to get his backpack and coat from the table.

I looked over at the crowd and said, "I think we are all set." And we walked out. I didn't sign him out. I didn't look back. The bell had sounded, and kids were starting to move around us in the hallway. We blended in and made our way to the parking lot and we headed home.

A few days later we had an emergency team meeting to

discuss Jack's recent incident. Apparently, Jack was taken to the subset room after he became frustrated by getting two problems wrong on a math paper. When he was brought to the subset room, another child was deescalating inside, so he went into the conference room next door instead. Jack commented on the loud noises coming from the room. The child was yelling, and they heard items being thrown against the wall. After a few minutes Jack appeared to have gotten back into the green zone, so he returned to class, only to have another flare-up later in the day. Going into the subset room to cool down, he noticed the mess from the other child. Jack became visibly upset about the state of the room and said, "I didn't do this!" When the social worker tried to address him, she wedged her foot in between the door, he pushed on it, pinching her foot. She told him that he had, "popped the top off," as labeled in his plan, which meant the red zone. As outlined in his earning chart, if he had a red behavior, there was no going back, no time earned for electronics.

"With all due respect, taking Jack back and forth from conference room to a subset room that was already destroyed, was yanking his chain. The subset room is a room for calming and for him to feel safe. This was not what he expected to see. He thought he was being blamed for what had happened and by alerting him that he had 'blown the top off,' there was no redemption. No reinforcement to be gained," Mike said to the group of school professionals during the team meeting.

"But his behavior seemed more deliberate. It was as if he was looking for hollow spots in the wall to find the electrical cord. He did manage to pop a couple of ceiling tiles out and he pulled the phone wire out, disconnecting service to the room next to his," Jennifer Booth said.

"At 3:20, after Nicole came and we were waiting him out, he looked at the clock and calmed down, as if he knew it was time to go home," Mrs. Damon added.

"What we need to flush out here is the *true antecedent*. I have been saying this time and time again…the antecedent is Jack's perfectionism. It is a challenge to measure perfectionism as an underlying cause, because it can be subtle, and observations are more subjective. It can be hard to pin down. What we have seen is Jack's criticalness toward other kids, taking on the role of the rule enforcer of his classroom. He struggles with accepting corrections, like how he responded to his grade on the math quiz. His resistance to taking a yellow break involves being seen as the kid who needs to take time out. Another example is his lack of tolerance of peers with visible disabilities and not wanting to be associated with them," Caroline said passionately. "THIS is the common thread between his behavioral episodes. This comes from his autism. Mrs. Sinclair, have you noticed if his anxiety level has increased in the classroom?" Caroline said, pivoting in Jack's teacher's direction.

"We have. It does seem to vary. The end of the day is harder for him, as is any unstructured time, or changes in our schedule," Mrs. Sinclair said.

"There seems to be a lot of time in between incidents," Mr. Wall said.

"With high functioning autism, sometimes he can access his skills, while other times he can't. It depends on what the variables are, what is impacting him within the environment or his day," Jennifer Booth responded.

"We need to discuss transport. The current procedure is not only challenging, it's also not safe. We only have two staff members who are trained and able to transport him and next year, the state protocol will be changing. His current BIP and our de-escalation procedures of the subset room will not be in compliance with the new regulations. And, Jack will be going to a new school next year. There are a lot of things to work through before next fall," Mr. Wall said.

It was decided that the two behaviorists would work together on adding reinforcement into his day and eliminating the all or nothing component of the current system. We would revisit the BIP and talk in depth about transition to the new Burbridge elementary school at the June team meeting, only a few weeks away. I was relieved to hear Caroline and Jennifer would be working together on the plan and reward system. Caroline had a keen eye and understood Jack and his flavor of autism. She has had the opportunity to work with many kids who presented behaviors like Jack. Her company was called in when kids were clearing desks, running from schools and had become combative. Some of them, like Jack, were not fully diagnosed, or worse, misdiagnosed.

Once in a phone conversation, Caroline said we were pioneers, blazing a trail for an understanding and creative programming concept for kids who presented like Jack. Hearing this made me weep, because it felt like a blessing and a burden. I deeply wanted Jack to be seen, valued and given an education that served all of his needs. I wanted a whole child approach to learning, which is part of the Montessori Philosophy, part of my educational beliefs. But in a public-school system, it just might be an impossible dream—at least for Jack. Maybe an increase of support and supervision would help as we finished the year…but what about his new school in the fall? He would be in another transition with new staff, which was concerning. I made a mental note to jot down questions to bring to his teacher, Mrs. Sinclair, for my parent-teacher conference. Maybe she would have a better idea of the landscape we would be moving into, specifically from someone who was non-administrative, and on the ground floor of the district's restructuring of the schools.

There had been a palpable buzz vibrating through the school system for several months. The Bradford school was closing due to age (costs of repairs needed were into the millions) and enrollment numbers had gone down in the past decade. The town had two other large elementary schools, Webster and Pinehurst. It had been determined the Webster School, which Jack attended, would house the preschool program up through second grade. Pinehurst would house third grade through sixth. Burbridge High School housed grades 7 and 8 in a separate wing. All of the kids who had attended Bradford (Jack's former school) would be enrolled in Pinehurst next fall. Kids who knew him at Bradford would be in the same building and I couldn't help but wonder what it would be like for him.

As I listened to Mrs. Sinclair that afternoon during our spring conference, I felt grateful Jack had experienced such a dedicated teacher. She focused on the positive, listing obstacles Jack had overcome and excelled at this year. And there had been many, despite the last few months of intermittent behaviors.

"Thank you for the kind words," I said, brushing away the tear from my cheek.

"Jack has been able to gain so much over the past two years I have been with him and I am so impressed by his resiliency and determination. It is an asset of his character," she said smiling. "In terms of next year, I wanted to bring up a couple of suggestions for you to advocate for as he moves into a different school. This year, I had to speak up to get time with the school behaviorist, Jennifer. She would stop in and discuss Jack during classroom hours. She didn't spend a lot of time observing Jack either, as she was stretched between three schools, and relied on our observations to guide her. I spoke up and was able to arrange consult time with Jennifer outside of the classroom, but my fear is that not everyone would do that," Mrs. Sinclair said candidly.

"Thank you for the insight," I said.

"She has been more involved since I self-advocated, and when his behaviors began to flare up, she came in more frequently. When things are going smoothly, well, she puts her energy into other cases," Mrs. Sinclair shrugged.

"And Jack needs to be monitored in those times when he is doing well. Antecedents can be elusive. Speaking of monitoring, do you know who the social worker will be at the Pinehurst School?" I asked.

"Last I heard, the social worker from Bradford would be assigned to Pinehurst," Mrs. Sinclair said.

"That is a huge concern. He was not only ineffective, he was a trigger," I said in a reactive tone as my heart sank inside my chest wondering how the transition work. "Who will be Jack's teacher next year? Do you have the assignments yet?" I blurted out.

"No. They are still configuring staff and rooms. To be honest, it's hard not knowing where we will be, or who we will be teaching with. It's been a taxing process for the teachers, as this redistricting has been discussed for years and now that it is finally happening, there are still so many details needed to be ironed out…I mean, maybe Mr. Earle won't be the social worker. Every day something changes…" her voice drifted as she looked at me.

"But I was told we should be getting the final names of the teachers next week," she said, after she read the stress in my brow.

As I drove home from the meeting with Jack's teacher, my mind was cluttered with fear and self-doubt, not about Jack's abilities, but maybe us pushing a regular setting had been wrong? Maybe Jack was not a good fit for a public school after all…

PERFECTION, MISSTEPS AND JOY

*A*lthough it was Saturday, I had taken the morning to gather notes and assemble questions for the team transition meeting schedule for next week. I had spoken to his specialists and had the information from the parent-teacher conference to discuss with Jane as we would, once again, formulate a plan for Jack. The weekend before was Memorial Day and the kids had spent time at Mike's family Lake house, visiting with cousins and putting in the docks for the season. The time spent up north was filled with icy dips in the water for brave ones, games of manhunt played well beyond dark, and the echo of late-night giggles from the children's bunkroom.

Weekends spent away were gifts. For us, it was like hitting the pause button on the reality of work, IEP plans and upcoming meetings and responsibilities. But it was more than that. It was time for play. Time to run a bit wild and to be ourselves. Sometimes, having a longer rope, more freedom and less structure, was hard for Jack. We set boundaries and created a schedule for the day to help anchor him, but over the years there had been a couple occasions when Jack had missteps. What I am beginning to understand after all these years, is that missteps *were expected behavior.*

We had spent a lot of time drilling into Jack's programming, as well as our family language about unexpected behavior: essentially, that it was wrong. But, wasn't it wrong to expect perfection? Had we curbed Jack's behavior to the point where we expected him to be perfect? In having time to relax, I let go of some of the residue from the past several months. I felt as though I was sinking into a different place. I wasn't denying the past, or the missteps by Jack, us and the people who worked with him. I needed to hit the pause button, to remember we were a family. We are love. We deserve normalcy in our everyday lives.

Riding the wave from the previous weekend, on that Saturday, I put aside the notes for Jane, the baskets of laundry, and the piles of mail, and we took the night for ourselves.

We traveled to see a double feature at the drive-in located further down Cape Cod. The older boys had plans, but the rest of us piled into the minivan with snacks, bug-spray, and bedding to get cozy in while watching the films. It was always a late night at the drive-in, but on a weekend it was fine. We broke bedtime curfews. We were rebels.

"Oh my God, mom! Did you see that? HOW, is that possible?!" Jack's voice exploded in disbelief as he raised his hand over his head nearly knocking over Aidan.

"Jack! I can't see!" Aidan exclaimed with a soft shove, pressing his shoulder into Jack's ribcage.

"Now, that's a knee slapper!" Jack said loudly. "Hey, Aidan, you want some candy?" Jack said without skipping a beat.

Little blue creatures with white hats danced across the screen. Laughter and surprised voices boomed with delight. Popcorn was eaten by the handful and candy consumed at an alarming rate, but I didn't care. I let it go. I let go of having to be "on" all the time. I let go of having to be the ruler, controller and the tracker of all things said and done. I let go of the lofty expectations I set for myself in every small detail of my life. Instead, I allowed the mess. The laughter. The spontaneous excursion to an outdoor movie an hour away. I felt profound gratitude fill my heart. I placed one hand on my chest and closed my eyes, taking in the chaos and sweetness of the moment, I allowed the labels to fall away and pure acceptance and love to flow through me as I was fully present.

I was on the verge of an internal shift. I could see the edge glimmer, almost winking at me, as I got a glimpse of it. Was it joy? Or freedom? Or was it both neatly woven together?

Days passed by and before I knew it, we were sitting at the team meeting to plan Jack's transition. The meeting got off to a rocky start when we saw Jack's former social worker had been invited to attend the meeting, even though we had strongly requested his attendance be excused. Mike spoke up and asked that it be written into the meeting notes that Mr. Earle wouldn't have any contact with or give any treatment to Jack as Mike and I felt Earle was a danger to our son due to his previous interactions with him at the Bradford School. Mike didn't want to have to state this, specifically in front of Mr. Earle, but as we spoke about transition and as Mr. Earle was the social worker at the new school Jack would be attending in September, our hand was forced.

After the rumbling subsided, Mr. Rafferty moved to outline Jack's current crisis protocol. Mrs. Damon was named as his crisis manager, but since she wasn't transitioning to the higher grades, she wouldn't be going over with Jack next year. This left either Mr. Earle, or they would need to hire another social worker. At the very least, someone else would need to be in charge of his crisis plan. Conversations about safety, transportation logistics and the anticipated changes in state regulations were exchanged. An hour into the meeting more questions than answers seemed to be unearthed. Many uncertainties of not only staffing, but bigger issues of policy and safety had risen to the surface.

"In your professional opinion, do you think Jack can be successful at the Pinehurst School?" Mr. Rafferty asked Jennifer Booth.

"With all of these unknown variables, I hate to say it, but I think we would be setting him up for failure. If he was staying with the current team at the same school, it would be a different story," Jennifer responded, seemingly disheartened.

"Do you agree?" Mr. Rafferty said as he looked over at Mr. Wall, Jack's current principal.

"Yes. I think it would be unfair to Jack, and I think I can speak for all of us at the Webster School by saying even in spite of his recent behaviors, he has come so very far in the last couple of years," Mr. Wall said with kind eyes.

"What we have here is the perfect storm. Jack should be placed in a public school, but in light of the current shifts within our district, I cannot say this would be a good transition for him.

I fear we will be in a reactive position, instead of a proactive position. I think we need to look at out-of-district placement for Jack." Mr. Rafferty said.

As I looked around the table of teaching staff, administration, specialized educators and support personnel, I saw all of the faces who had helped Jack on his journey. So many of them worked tirelessly for his success. Yes, mistakes and miscommunication had happened, at times, to Jack's detriment. But that was in the past. I didn't feel angry, only deeply disappointed we had arrived in this position. I knew the recommendation was the best answer, but I felt defeated. I wondered how I would give Jack the news about moving him to another school out of town. Away from his friends and the public school he had anticipated he'd be attending in the fall. Would he feel like he failed?

Above all, I didn't want him to feel like a failure. I wanted to focus on the successes. I was tired of looking at his lack, the ways he was different. As the meeting wrapped up, we had the names of three specialized schools. The nearest was thirty-five minutes away and the other two were close to an hour drive. Mike and I collected ourselves, thanked the team and told Mr. Rafferty we would be in touch.

Over the next couple of weeks, while Jack and his brothers were finishing up the school year, we were gathering information about the prospective collaborative schools. The Mayflower Collaborative, which was the closest, had restructured their education system and were presently taking grades 5 and up. Jack would be in fourth grade in September. One down, two to go. The Redding School was located near Rhode Island, so it was the furthest. Although the school had smaller classroom sizes and had the specialized supports Jack needed, they didn't have behavioral support to work through Jack's behavior plan. One more down.

The last collaborative school included a program called Rising Stars, which was specifically geared toward kids with anxiety, high-functioning autism, and ADHD. They had a dedicated cluster of rooms for behavior de-escalation and calming. In addition, they had a behavior team. If a child became disruptive and was unable to calm in the classroom setting, the "B-Team" would come in and escort the child to one of the rooms where he could regain his composure. Tools and strategies were implemented and there was even a separate sensory room they could access once they were ready. Small classroom size and student-teacher ratios, along with group sessions for social pragmatics and self-regulation skill building were done in each classroom weekly. Jack would be receiving more support than he had in the past, which was great, but we had concerns about the level of his academics. How would they fit it all into a six-and-a-half-hour day?

When Mike and I met with the director of the Rising Stars program, we brought our concerns with us. It was clear from meeting Jessica that she was dedicated and knowledgeable not only about the children she serviced and her staff, but honest about the areas where we would need to get creative, adding more educational components into Jack's schedule. We found her honesty and ability to work with us reassuring. Even though the school was the last one on our list, we felt it was the right one for our son.

IN A PRIVATE MEETING with Mr. Rafferty, Jane, Mike and I, we signed paperwork to get Jack transferred to the Rising Stars program for September. Even though they offered a summer program, we had thought it would be a lot for him to digest. Instead we secured summer services through Atlas Educational Services and Caroline was named to be his BCBA for the remainder of the current IEP. Jack's new school didn't have a designated BCBA; they used a universal behavior plan that was executed by the social workers and staff. There was a behaviorist in the building, but she worked primarily with the high school students. Jessica, the program director of Rising Stars, reassured us her staff would work collaboratively with Caroline and add components of Jack's BIP into the classroom.

I was feeling good, but a bit nervous. I was relieved he'd be in a safer environment, but worried he'd learn new worse behaviors. Caroline and her staff worked on getting Jack ready for transitioning into his new school. Her biggest concern was van transport. She wanted to make sure his reinforcement plan was dense enough in the area of school and transport. We worked in a high rate of rewards for screen time earned by positive behaviors at school and on the van. He also earned prizes when he had six successful days of non-red behavior (in school or at home). These prizes earned were items he picked: highly desired books or Minecraft figures, which reinforced expected behavior.

Caroline went into the Rising Stars program to discuss his current plan and the earn sheets. She also met with Jessica to discuss transport and get an understanding of how dismissal worked and to trouble shoot worst case scenarios. At the meeting with Rafferty, Jane had requested a bus monitor be on his IEP to ensure another layer of safety, which everyone agreed upon.

As the end of summer was fast approaching, Jack, Aidan and I, took to the beach to enjoy one last day. We met Faith and her sons there. Spending the day with friends would be great for the kids and it gave Faith and me time to catch up. We had remained close, but as our children grew and stretched themselves, life became busier, with less time spent at the playground pushing them on swings or chasing them around. Driving to activities, appointments and shopping for food and supplies had become the new normal for both of us.

"I am feeling pretty good about Jack's new school," I said.

Faith nodded. "I know last spring was challenging for all of you. This will be so good for him. I didn't mention Jack's new school to the kids, as I wasn't sure if he was okay with it yet," she said almost shyly.

"Oh, yes. He's telling people. He seems happy about going, which is a relief. Jack and I toured the school and we met his teacher already," I said.

My mind circled on her reservations to talk to her kids about Jack's placement. It made me think about how we tended to walk on eggshells around Jack. Sometimes it was needed, maybe because plans were not finalized yet. As I sat with the feeling, I realized it was an old one. Probably from my upbringing, of where we didn't share things outside of the house: a "don't tell the neighbors" type of thing. Certainly, that message was not unique to my family; it was part of the white-picket-fence culture. I am sure Faith's goal was to be respectful, but the familiarity of the feeling reminded me of how some people perceived behavioral kids and the families who raised them. I know this, because I had perceptions about families with kids who acted out before I had Jack. But I just didn't understand. Now I do.

I understand not everything is as it seems. Behavior is the tip of the iceberg, a symptom of something bigger lying under the surface. There is always a reason for a behavior. Working with my son and other kids with regulation issues gifted me the opportunity to really see them, to seek clarity in what was their truth, as opposed to focusing on the outward manifestation. My child was not his behavior. He was someone who struggled, who had both diagnosed and undiagnosed disabilities, which made it a challenge to access traditional education without accommodations. Instead of seeing my child or anyone else's as a "problem," I saw them with compassionate eyes. They were the brave ones, shouting louder and louder to be heard. Jack taught me to listen and demanded that all of us to go beyond what was seen to look deeper still. As I answered the call, helping to forge a path to unearth what was underneath his behaviors, I began to understand. Jack offered me a different lens through which to see the world. And gratefully, I took it. I began to care less about how other people perceived us, our family, our choices, because it didn't matter. Their opinions didn't make or break us. The labels given to Jack were derived by something he did, not who he was. Inside the heart of compassion, unconditional love reigned; Jack was love and love was what mattered. Love was the place we returned to over and over again.

EVERYTHING WAS IN PLACE: backpacks filled with school supplies, and lunchboxes were stacked next to the fridge. Jack's IEP, along with his BIP, were in place and the team was connected and on board. All the pieces were assembled, except the pieces in my heart. Hearing the hesitation in Faith brought to my attention the fear I was holding on to; fear about what other people thought; fear Jack would interpret the school change as a step backwards; fear of the unknowns that a new school environment would bring. As we sat being warmed by the sun, watching our group of boys run and jump off the side of the marsh into the creek, I laid out my fears to Faith. I took a breath in between sentences. She looked at me and placed her hand on my arm.

"Are you carrying around guilt about Jack?" she asked.

"What do you mean?"

"It sounds like you feel like it's your fault, like you are feeling responsible for Jack being at this point in his life," Faith said.

"Sometimes I think, did we make the wrong choice two-plus years ago? Was it all for nothing? Did we make it hard on him, by trying to fit him into a system, a school culture, which wasn't in his best interest? So, yes, I guess I do have guilt. I am not entirely sure I can trust myself in light of pushing so hard for a public education that in the end, didn't work for him," I said.

"You gave Jack the biggest gift by pushing him and the professionals! Don't you see? You gave Jack dignity. You provided an opportunity for him to stretch himself in ways he wouldn't have been able to in a different environment. By both you and Mike standing up for his rights, keeping people accountable, you created change. I guarantee you, the experience of working with and for Jack, shifted people's viewpoints of how they see kids with similar diagnoses."

"And that was what I wanted. I wanted Jack to be seen, to be valued, to be supported. And he was, but the pressure and the environment I think was too overwhelming for him." I said.

"But you and Mike tried. If you guys didn't push; if you didn't give him the opportunity of a fresh start, after enlisting the proper supports, you would have always wondered if it was possible…"

———

Labor Day weekend was designated a "work weekend" up at the lake house. Docks that had seemingly been put into place only weeks ago, were being pulled out and stored for the next summer season. Boats were pulled ashore and winterized. On Sunday, the people from the many homes on the dirt road, maybe twenty of them, gathered together for coffee and "road crew," when they patched holes in the road and did other jobs to help maintain the community.

This had become my weekend of solitude. The boys went up to the lake and I stayed home, hitting my own pause button by filling my spiritual cup. I was grateful to have two days of freedom, answering only to myself. It was a bit like winning the mommy lottery.

On this particular weekend, I knew I had work to do: inner work. I had been mulling over the conversation Faith and I had and the mixture of feelings it had brought up. I needed to embrace this change with every fiber of my being. To become excited about Jack's new beginning and allow it to flow freely. But I needed space to get there. I had to become quiet, to slow down and be in nature. I needed time to write and journal. I needed opportunities to breathe and feel. It was the only way though the haze and noise of my brain. Part of me wanted to resist the inner work of my feelings, but it was where truth and clarity lived. Unless I wanted to stay stuck in the fear, guilt and mistrust, I needed to dive inside.

Something magical happened when I allowed myself to flow. I let go of resisting change, internal or external. I softened into a place where the words I scribed poured out of me: uncensored, organic, raw. That was where the truth lived. I peeled back the layers of guilt, shame, unworthiness, responsibly, and fear. None of these aspects were really mine; I had taken them on…now it was time to call bullshit on them. It was time to release them and stand in the truth.

What is my truth? I am worthy. I make good decisions. I am capable, loving and strong. My intentions come from a deep love for my children and family. I am not my missteps or mistakes. I am on a lifelong journey of discovery, blazing a trail with compassion and care. I am beautifully imperfect. I am not responsible for every component of life. Trusting in myself, my intentions and the universe, brings comfort that I am not going this alone.

My mind drifted back and I saw the faces of the people who had shown up over the past several years. I couldn't have better orchestrated these people who arrived to assist us, from our "first responders," Jane, Robin, Maggie, Caroline and her ABA team, to the neuropsychologist who brought us the diagnosis, to the public-school professionals who were willing to roll-up their sleeves and get to work.

When Jack was at Bradford and his behaviors had spiked— he was so big and loud, he didn't fall through the cracks. Jack demanded to be seen. In hindsight, running out of the building was the catalyst for understanding his needs. The twist and turns on the journey had been necessary, as they had taught and challenged us to become more than we thought we could be. Every step I had taken had brought me to this moment. No matter how rocky or smooth the pathway was, as I looked back, I could see there was a bigger plan at play.

As I stood in the forest near my home on that weekend, I knew it was time to surrender. I used my breath to settle into my body. With arms stretched out wide I opened my heart. In the solitude of nature, I heard the flutter of wings, the racing feet of squirrels on branches overhead and the monotone sound of the crickets ushering in an early evening. A smile crossed my face as I realized my place in the world. Of all the workings, the creation of living was happening in every corner, and in every second. It made me feel humble and exquisitely small.

A breeze blew into the grove of trees. When the coolness of the air rushed by, I felt grace move through me and I was bathed in peace…

"All is well…all is well," I said out loud for all and no one to hear.

EPILOGUE

*J*ack transitioned into Rising Stars beautifully. He has been attending the program for several years. In a smaller classroom with therapeutic supports, Jack has thrived. Teachers and staff members often comment on Jack's ability to bring kids together, as he has taken on leadership roles with enthusiasm and an inclusive attitude. This past year, Jack worked in a small group with peers on perspective taking. His involvement in this group deepened Jack's understanding of others and how they feel. Jack has been able to generalize this awareness at home and in our community. Although Jack still gets caught up in being perfect, being part of a school that cultivates kindness, and by watching peers make mistakes too, he has been able to accept not only other people's differences, but also his own.

As a part of Jack's goals for independence, he has been working toward an increased level of self-awareness. It is important as Jack matures that he understands how autism impacts in his daily way of living. Although his autism has many classic features, the way it manifests in his life is not the exact same way it does in others. Understanding his own body and how his mind processes information is a key component for Jack's continued success. He has been guided by professionals to look at his strengths and at the areas he requires support and because of this has been proactive and advocates for his needs. Jack doesn't see himself as broken or deficient. He sees himself as a budding historian who may need a little help along the way as he reaches towards his dreams. He has been one of my biggest teachers and has taught me more about resilience and self-love than I ever imagined. He has taught me to believe, to trust. And, most importantly, to never underestimate the human spirit and how transformational love can be.

We have been able to work with his new team in a collaborative and respectful way. Jack is constantly evolving on all levels, so we pay attention to any flags that begin to rise. Jack has been able to regulate his body and emotions within the program and in the home environment. Red zone behaviors bubble up infrequently and he de-escalates quickly. Jack is rarely taken out of class for behavior interventions. He is able to articulate why he is feeling sad or frustrated and uses strategies within the classroom to come back to the green zone. He has come a long way in feeling and dealing with his emotions and I believe having a smaller setting with supports has been instrumental in his progression.

After I left my teaching position, I shifted into working with special needs students. I studied behavioral science and became a

Board Certified Behavior Technician. The specialized school provided an opportunity for me to build a new preschool program. I created a hybrid preschool program, blending Montessori teachings and philosophies with behavioral supports. I had come full circle, able to bring Montessori to the special needs community within a small supportive setting. In 2017, I felt called to leave that position to focus on bringing this book, *A Life Suspended*, into the world.

As a mom who had struggled with the chaos and confusion of having a child with disabilities, I felt moved to share my story. At my lowest points, I felt ashamed, shunned and alone. This made me feel hopeless and overwhelmed. Over the past years, I have heard countless stories of children and families who have endured this pathway to education. Most of the time, people have asked me about our experience, looking for connection, advice, but mostly understanding. Jack's story wasn't unique. Every time I spoke to someone who was in the midst of the process, my heart broke, because I remembered. Although I couldn't wave a wand and make it better, I felt in a small way by sharing my experience with kindness and compassion, I could give them hope.

In so many ways, living a life suspended has changed me. Jack may have been suspended from school, but over time we found ourselves suspended in love. There was always someone, somewhere, who stepped up. Many helpful hands guided us and him along this uncharted path. Living a life suspended has not only taught me to trust and to let go; it has shown me where my strengths and reserves lie. The lens through which I see the world has become clearer and my capacity for compassion has expanded beyond the boundaries of my heart. Even with the tears, I am profoundly grateful for the experience, as it cracked me wide open. I hope to remain in rarified air, mindful of how far we've all come, and excited for what is yet to be.

ACKNOWLEDGMENTS

Jack Donovan for your bravery, resilience and willingness to
share your story. Thank you for being a power of example in my
life and in the lives of all around you.

Mike whose love, attention and unwavering devotion was the
rock which kept us steady during the most crucial moments.
Your belief in Jack and in our family, empowered me to find a
way through multiple obstacles. Your encouragement to write
and publish *A Life Suspended* (*ALS*) was influential in its
creation. I am forever grateful for you.

Jack's brothers for him to be loved and cared for by you was
essential for his recovery from trauma. It gave him a safe place to
learn how to self-regulate and create a new way of moving
though the world. I deeply appreciate your willingness to understand Jack and his differences. Thank you for standing up for

him, being his advocate with peers who didn't "get him," and above all for being his friend.

Patrick the eldest of our crew who stepped in during difficult times. Your readiness to help, to understand and to see Jack with love has meant the world to us all. *Kieran* your sensitivity and kind heart has shown me a wider lens to view others through, and as my perspective has changed, my capacity for compassion has expanded. *Aidan* you have been a good brother and friend to Jack, even when it was hard. Having you in his life has had a profound impact.

First Responders, you were the lifeline we desperately needed. The educational advocate who taught us how to navigate the educational system. The BCBA and her team who were in the trenches every day shaping Jack's behavior. The mental health counselor and the occupational therapist who worked with Jack on gaining emotional tools and life skills. Every single one of you went the extra mile. My gratitude runs deep and wide for the time and dedication you gave to Jack, to me and to our family. You were instrumental in getting him where he is today.

The Team of educational and therapeutic professionals who consistently gathered around numerous conference tables to talk about Jack. Your willingness to listen, to be open to suggestions and to problem solve was essential. Sometimes we didn't see eye-to-eye. Sometimes things ended in frustration. But, in the end we knew we all had the same goal; for Jack to succeed.

Friends and loved ones who gave their unconditional love to

Jack and our family. You didn't judge, only listened. You showed up and believed in Jack's unlimited potential. Thank you for being in the "ring" with us. For letting me sob on your shoulder and bend your ear for countless hours. In many ways you were the sustenance I needed to power through. You filled my cup when it was empty, and my heart is eternally full.

Ron Suskind for your inspirational memoir, *Life Animated*, your personal story about your autistic son Owen. Thank you for sharing your vulnerability and love for you son with me. Your audiobook played and played as I drove around Cape Cod. You gave me hope. You helped me believe.

John Elder Robinson before I knew about my son's autism, I read your story. *Look Me in the Eye* was a powerful account of what it was like to grow up without an autism diagnosis. It allowed me to see autism through an autistic man's eyes. Thank you for bravely sharing your experience with the world and gifting so many of us a different perspective.

AANE Asperger / Autism Network gave us our first introduction to being parents of a child with autism. AANE provided information and support during a critical time in our lives. Thank you for being there and helping so many families in New England.

Darla Bruno for your expertise in editing *ALS* early on and looking at the story as a whole. Thank you for your input during the developmental stages.

Kat Szmit for your expertise in line editing *ALS*. I am grateful for your attention to detail and making the book even better!

Kate Conway for your experience and guidance during the publication process! Creating a book cover that "pops" and sharing marketing tools with me. First, you made the idea of becoming an indie author seem reachable, then you helped me achieve it!

For the Children and Families, I have known, met and worked with over the years. You have been my inspiration and motivation to get this story told. This story is for you, the ones who came before, and the ones who will come after.

A LIFE SUSPENDED BOOK CLUB
DISCUSSION QUESTIONS

• Which character or situation in the story resonated most with you? Why?

• Perfectionism is a theme for both mother and son in the book, how do you see this in society? In yourself?

• At one point the author says, "With every new diagnosis, I kept thinking they didn't capture it all. At times I got the impression that people thought that I was on a witch hunt to find something that was not there. I felt alone, and at times, crazy." Have you experienced this, personally or in advocating for someone else? How did you navigate listening to your intuition? What did it teach you?

• As a way to reduce her stress level and bring balance back into her life, the author spends time becoming grounded in both old and new activities. What kinds of activities do you use to de-stress or for self-care? Is there a new activity you would like to add to your practice, if so what?

• The author became hyper-focused on what was missing from Jack's skillset and programing. Over time, this colored how she viewed her own life, looking towards the lack, rather than what was in abundance. She began to note what she was grateful for. Write down three aspects of your life you are grateful for and share them with the group.

• In *A Life Suspended*, mother and son become enmeshed, as their stories are interwoven due to their circumstances. The author became consumed with of the components of caring and advocating for Jack. By fighting for Jack, she was given opportunities to step into her own power. She found her voice and her courage. Reflect on a time in your own life when you were faced with a challenge. How did you handle it? Did it carry over into other areas of your life?

• What is the difference between guilt and shame? How did these feelings impact the characters and fuel their actions?

• What was your biggest "take away," from reading *A Life Suspended*?

• One of the themes in the book is control and many of the characters grapple with it. The police officer, Mr. Raffety, and Mrs. Paulson tried to enforce control with their title or station. Jack struggled to regulate his body and control his emotions. The parents and advocates tried to arrange all these pieces in what they hoped was the best way for Jack. Eventually the author realized fear was the antecedent of control, and control was an illusion. She learned she had very little power over what Jack would do, or choices others would make, or what the future would bring. What aspect of control in the story spoke the loudest to you? Why?

• In the book, one of the therapeutic activities Jack worked on was a Success Book, in which he included photos and drawings of milestones where he felt he achieved a goal (no matter how big or small). If you were creating a Success Book, what would you add to it?

• Labels both hindered and helped Jack throughout the story. Labels can be necessary for gaining access to much-needed services but can also place limits on people. As individuals, we can utilize labels to define who we are and what we do, but this can also be limiting. If you took away all of your labels/titles who would you be? What descriptors would you use to define you?

• *A Life Suspended*, is used as a metaphor, as Jack was expelled from school and Nicole's life was placed on hold. Over time they realized, even during the hardest moments, they were suspended, suspended in love. From Jack's "first responders," to the spiritual breadcrumbs laid out for the author, they were held in love. Has there been a time in your life where you look back and saw love step in? How has that knowing shifted your perspective?

ABOUT THE AUTHOR

Nicole (Hendrick) Donovan is a former Montessori educator who worked with a variety of students with various needs. During her teaching career, she created a Montessori preschool classroom which integrated neurotypical and non-neurotypical learners. After her experience with her son, she became an ABA therapist and worked closely with children diagnosed with autism and their families. In 2017, Nicole, shifted her energy and focused on her writing career.

Nicole lives on Cape Cod with her husband Mike, four sons and an assortment of rescued cats and dogs. Both Nicole and Mike have continued to work with Jack's team in supporting his development in all areas. Nicole is a public speaker and facilitator whose passion is to bring awareness and self-healing through personal storytelling. For information about upcoming events or to read from her blog catalog, visit www.nhdwrites.com.

Made in the USA
Middletown, DE
24 December 2020